Country Friends® Go Quilting
Book 2

They like to spend long afternoons cruising the antique shops, folding & unfolding, ooohing-and-aaahing over the old quilts. They love snappy red-and-white Log Cabins, soft pastel Wedding Rings & vivid patchworks. They spend happy hours at the corner craft store contemplating the calicos & homespuns... with a side-trip, of course, for Double Fudge Sundaes, heavy on the whipped cream & sprinkles!

They're the Country Friends®, three-of-a-kind who love all things country & quilted: Kate, all thumbs when it comes to sewing on buttons, can't get her hands on enough of them for crafting & collecting... Holly, who leans toward the finer things in life like stacks & stacks of homespun fabric & quilting patterns... and Mary Elizabeth, who always has at least six projects underway and another dozen in mind! And don't forget faithful old Spotty ⌐ he tags along in every chapter just to see what happens next!

The Country Friends® have pieced together a quilting adventure as enchanting as an old Friendship quilt. You're welcome to come along... there's always room for another Country Friend!

Country Friends® Go Quilting
Book 2

Content and Artwork by **Gooseberry Patch Company**

LEISURE ARTS
Vice President and Editor-in-Chief: Sandra Graham Case
Executive Director of Publications: Cheryl Nodine Gunnells
Director of Designer Relations: Debra Nettles
Publications Director: Kristine Anderson Mertes
Design Director: Cyndi Hansen
Editorial Director: Susan Frantz Wiles
Photography Director: Lori Ringwood Dimond
Licensed Product Coordinator: Lisa Truxton Curton

EDITORIAL STAFF

EDITORIAL
Managing Editor: Alan Caudle
Senior Editor: Linda L. Garner

TECHNICAL
Managing Editor: Cheryl Johnson
Senior Technical Writer: Lisa Lancaster

FOODS
Foods Editor: Celia Fahr Harkey, R.D.
Technical Assistant: Judy Millard

DESIGN
Designer: Linda Diehl Tiano
Craft Assistant: Lucy Beaudry

ART
Senior Art Director: Rhonda Hodge Shelby
Senior Production Artist: Lora Puls
Lead Artist: Elaine Wheat

Production Artists: Mark R. Potter and Dana Vaughn
Color Technician: Mark Hawkins
Staff Photographer: Russell Ganser
Staff Photography Stylists: Janna Laughlin
and Cassie Newsome
Publishing Systems Administrator: Becky Riddle
Publishing Systems Assistants: Myra S. Means
and Chris Wertenberger

PROMOTIONS
Associate Editor: Steven M. Cooper
Designer: Dale Rowett
Graphics Artist: Deborah Kelly

BUSINESS STAFF
Publisher: Rick Barton
Vice President, Finance: Tom Siebenmorgen
Director of Corporate Planning and Development:
Laticia Mull Cornett
Vice President, Retail Marketing: Bob Humphrey
Vice President, Sales: Ray Shelgosh
Vice President, National Accounts: Pam Stebbins
Director of Sales and Services: Margaret Reinold
Vice President, Operations: Jim Dittrich
Comptroller, Operations: Rob Thieme
Retail Customer Service Managers: Sharon Hall
and Stan Raynor
Print Production Manager: Fred F. Pruss

Softcover ISBN 1-57486-252-9

10 9 8 7 6 5 4 3 2

Contents

friendship is the golden thread that ties the heart of all the world.
– JOHN EVELYN 1620-1706 –

PATRIOTIC P*R*I*D*E*

Three cheers for the red, white & blue! Show your spirit with all-American touches year 'round! You may want to just add an accent piece, like our old-fashioned sampler wall hanging...or you can redecorate an entire room!

Patriotic Quilt, page 46; Patriotic Shams, page 47; Flag Pillow, page 48

*S*ponge white paint all over a miniature flowerpot. When dry, add red stripes around the rim and stencil blue stars on the base, then fill with little flags…an instant burst of all-American spirit!

Hooray for the USA!

Stars and Stripes Forever!

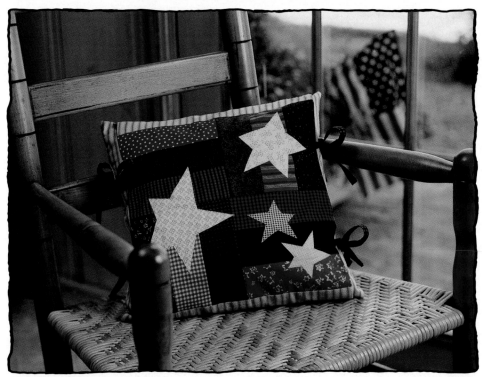

Star Pillow, page 48

We chose homespun prints in country shades of red, cream and blue to create the popular Dancing Star pattern on our patchwork quilt, pillow and table runner.

"My country, 'tis of thee,
Sweet land of liberty,
Of thee I sing;
Land where my fathers died,
Land of the Pilgrim's pride,
From every mountain side
Let freedom ring."

— Samuel F. Smith

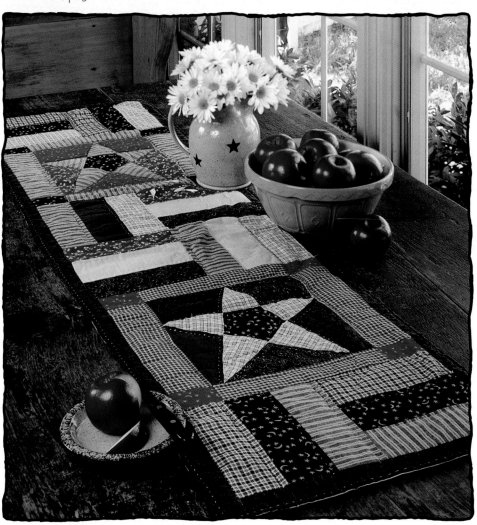

Dancing Star Table Runner, page 52

Dancing Star Quilt, page 51

America

is a land of wonders, in which everything is in constant motion and every change seems an improvement....

Alexis de Tocqueville

Decorate with red, white & blue for an outdoor gathering! Hang old-fashioned buntings along the porch railing and fill white baskets with red carnations, blue petunias and white daisies. Don't hide those beautiful quilts in the bedroom...drape them across your picnic table or on the backs of your rocking chair and garden swing.

There's no place like Home

There's no place like "home sweet home," especially when it's filled with lots of cozy, country touches…ours are oh-so simple! Because the appliqués are fused in place, the wall hanging and framed piece are a snap to make, and you can sew up a whole basketful of little hearts in no time!

"Home Sweet Home" Wall Hanging, page 55

"Home Sweet Home" Framed Piece, page 56; Stuffed Hearts, page 59

♥I know not why, but home is dearest. Cicero 106 - 43 B.C.

Do you have a collection of old buttons? Use a glue gun to easily attach some of the prettiest ones to a picture frame.

APPLE GOODNESS

Bright-red, crispy-crunchy and oh-so sweet…the country goodness of apples makes them a natural choice for this kitchen collection! Their delicious aroma will draw the whole family to the room when you stir up a batch of old-fashioned apple butter; while it's simmering, you can get started on our perky appliquéd wall hanging.

The Manner of giving is worth More than the gift.
— Pierre Corneille

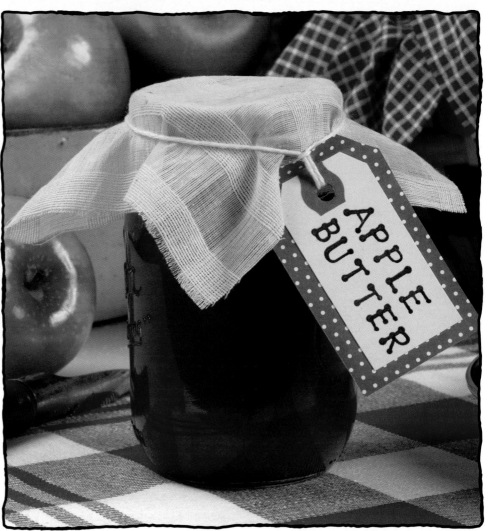

Apple Butter Jar, page 59

DAD'S SPICED APPLE BUTTER

This is an easy slow-cooker recipe that is good served on biscuits or muffins.

8 to 10 Rome, Braeburn or
    Granny Smith apples, peeled
    and quartered
1/2 c. apple juice or water
2 T. lemon juice
3/4 c. sugar
1 t. cinnamon
1/8 t. ground cloves
1/8 t. salt
1/8 t. ground allspice
1/8 t. nutmeg

Place apples in a slow cooker; add juice or water and lemon juice. Combine remaining ingredients in a small bowl; stir until blended. Add to apples; stir. Cover and cook on low 8 hours or on high 3 to 4 hours. Stir and mash apples occasionally throughout cooking time. When desired thickness, ladle apple butter into 6 hot, sterilized half-pint jars. Add lid and tighten down ring. Cool jars. Store in refrigerator.

Dayna Hansen
Junction City, OR

Apple Wall Hanging, page 59

Dress up your breakfast table! The stem on the apple-shaped place mat is actually a clever holder for the napkin "leaves." For a cheery centerpiece, fill a napkin-lined basket with an assortment of plump soft-sculpture apples.

During your next autumn bonfire, enjoy a warm and tasty apple treat! Slide an apple on a metal skewer and roast until warmed throughout. Slice and enjoy with caramel sauce or sprinkled with cinnamon and sugar.

Baked squash is delicious stuffed with a mixture of chopped apples, raisins, brown sugar and butter!

Soft-Sculpture Apples, page 61

12

Apple Place Mat and Napkin, page 62

APPLE CRUNCH MUFFINS
A delicious fall treat for breakfast at home or on the run!

1¹/₂ c. all-purpose flour
¹/₂ c. sugar
2 t. baking powder
¹/₂ t. salt
¹/₂ t. cinnamon
¹/₄ c. shortening
¹/₂ c. milk
1 egg, slightly beaten
1 c. Granny Smith apples,
    peeled and diced

TOPPING
¹/₄ c. brown sugar, packed
¹/₄ c. chopped walnuts
¹/₂ t. cinnamon

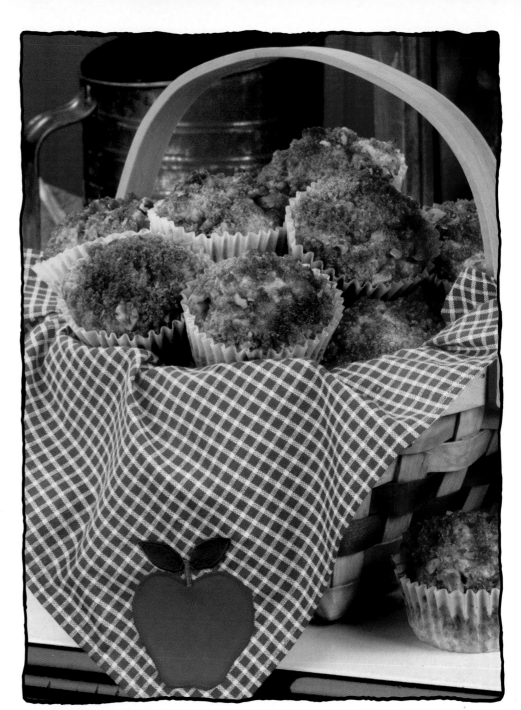

Apple Bread Cloth, page 62

Sift flour, sugar, baking powder, salt and cinnamon in mixing bowl. Cut in shortening until fine crumbs form. Combine milk and egg. Add to dry ingredients along with apples. Stir just until moistened. Spoon batter into muffin cups, filling two-thirds full. For topping, mix ingredients together. Sprinkle topping over batter. Bake at 375 degrees for 20 minutes or until golden. Makes 12.

I was 32 when I started cooking; up until then, I just ATE. – JULIA CHILD

- Make a family trip to an apple orchard ~ a picking expedition is a memory-maker.
- Green and red apples in a bowl are a beautiful sight to behold.
- Mary Elizabeth's kids love this harvest treat: Core an apple, fill it with peanut butter and top it with raisins.

Ticking dish towels and a checked bread cloth appliquéd with apples add a colorful, retro feel to any kitchen. Set out a basket of moist, spicy muffins for snacking!

Apple Appliquéd Hand Towels, page 64

Cheery Cherry Nursery

Greet baby with an "orchard" of appliquéd cherries…Mary Elizabeth's favorite! We combined traditional print fabrics with an open fruit-print plaid for a fresh, cheerful look that's suitable for both girls and boys. The adorable wall hanging features appliquéd blocks alternated with traditional Nine-Patches, and the crib set is easy to piece together.

Cheery Cherry Wall Hanging, page 64

Cheery Cherry Crib Quilt, page 67; Bumper Pads, page 70

Favorite Country Friends® baby gifts: A baby's cup, the softest blankie imaginable, personalized "Thank-You" notes printed with baby's name, a keepsake photo frame, a sterling locket engraved with baby's name and birthdate, a collection of classic lullabies on compact disc and a hand-painted toy box.

Babies
are always more
trouble
~than you thought~
and more
Wonderful.
─CHARLES OSGOOD─

Mother and baby will
be spending a lot of time
in the nursery, so make it
especially cozy and inviting.
Rocking baby will be even
more relaxing with a comfy
cushion for the rocking chair,
and the changing pad cover
can be easily removed
for washing.

*If you just can't bear to
pack away baby's extra-special
outfits, display them! They can be
mounted in a shadowbox frame or
clipped on a tiny clothesline…or
snippets of worn-out clothes can
be pieced together to make a
sweet quilt or wall hanging
full of memories.*

Chair Pad, page 70

Cheery Cherry Changing Pad Cover, page 72; Cheery Cherry Valance, page 73

*"A child should always say what's true
And speak when he is spoken to,
And behave mannerly at the table:
At least as far as he is able."*

— Robert Louis Stevenson

Why buy all-new furniture when you can hand down a treasured piece from your own childhood? It's easy to make everything coordinate! Simply paint the pieces the same color and cover with matching fabric. A colorful throw pillow completes the collection…for a boy, you could omit the ruffle and finish the pillow with a knife-edge, or add welting.

Fabric-Covered Dresser, page 73

Cheery Cherry Pillow, page 74

The good things in Life are not to be had SINGLY; but come to us with a MIXTURE.
— anonymous —

Fabric scraps can be used to create a photo frame, and it's oh-so easy! Find a flat, white wooden frame (or paint one), cut fabric strips a little narrower than the frame borders and fuse or glue in place. Glue big, bright buttons to the corners and add a bow, if you like.

"The best way to make children good is to make them happy."

— Oscar Wilde

Start a keepsake collection for a little one. You can use a toy box, trunk, blanket chest…it doesn't matter what you use, what's important is what's inside. Some ideas: Grandma's embroidered hankies, tried & true favorite recipes, a handed-down quilt, scrapbooks, special cards & letters and family photos.

Let It Snow!

If you just can't wait for the first snow of the season, you'll love our frosty friend! We made him into an appliquéd wall hanging and pillow, as well as a cuddly chenille doll.

Snowman Wall Hanging, page 75

Chenille Snowman, page 77

Enjoy a wintry day of play with your children! Bake and decorate cookies, make snow ice cream, build a snow fort or cut out paper snowflakes.

"Frosty, in a coat of red, with a scarf upon his head. A ball of snow from head to toe, before the springtime he must go!"

— Unknown

Snowman Pillow, page 80

Springtime Blossoms

Who can resist the appeal of a springtime garden? Come along with us and let Kate, Holly and Mary Elizabeth show you some of their all-time favorite floral patchwork patterns. Tulip fanciers will love reproducing this pretty antique coverlet...the blocks are positioned with the tulip tips together to create an intriguing design.

Tulip Quilt, page 81

Dogwood Quilt, page 82

One of the first flowering trees to bloom in the spring, the dogwood dots the forest with puffy clouds of pink and white. We just had to find a way to bring these beautiful blossoms indoors! Girls of all ages will enjoy our appliquéd quilt, pillow and wall hanging. Simple Nine-Patch blocks accent the corners of the wall hanging.

Fun fact: The dogwood is the state flower or tree of Virginia, North Carolina, New Jersey and Missouri, as well as the official provincial flower of British Columbia.

Dogwood Pillow, page 85; Dogwood Wall Hanging, page 86

To add a touch of spring anywhere, stitch up this trio of blossoming pillows. You could also use the patchwork blocks to make wall hangings, potholders or framed pieces...put your creative talents to work!

Dress your home for spring with fresh-cut flowers from your garden! Place vases overflowing with daffodils, lilacs and tulips on your kitchen table, mantel, stairsteps, sideboard and windowsills. You can even tuck a large basketful of flowers in an empty fireplace for a fresh springtime look!

Pot of Lilies Pillow, page 90; Grandmother's Flower Garden Pillow, page 89; Palm Leaf Pillow, page 87

She who kneels where violets grow
a thousand secret things shall know.
—OLD FOLK RHYME

28

*S*tacked on shelves, folded over one another to show off their colors and patterns or framing a single block; quilts are fun to decorate with!

Picture Perfect Quilts

Kate, Holly and Mary Elizabeth have a terrific idea for remembering all those special occasions…quilted wall hangings…a snap to make with color transfers of photographs and artwork! Choose any subject: an anniversary, the first day of school, a favorite holiday or family vacation.

Make a family photo calendar: Select snapshots for each month of the year and make color copies. You may want to use one photo per month, or you can make a collage for each month. Arrange and glue on a ready-made wall calendar, then fill in family birthdays, anniversaries and events. You can also take your photos to a print shop and let them make a custom-designed calendar for you.

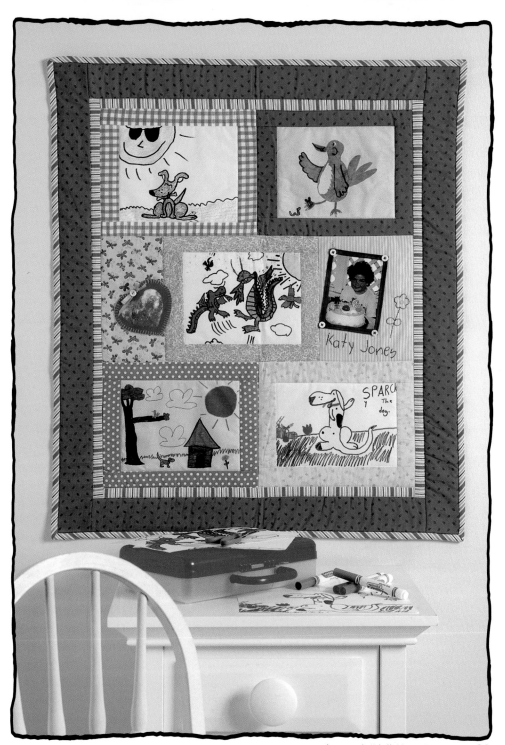

Artwork Wall Hanging, page 92

Anniversary Wall Hanging, page 93

Fireside Quilts

When the days turn brisk and chilly and the nights become longer, it's the perfect time to settle in beside the fire and stitch a warm, cozy quilt. Let the beautiful autumn colors be your inspiration as you select fabrics to re-create this antique Trip Around the World quilt…it's sure to be a cherished heirloom!

Trip Around the World Quilt, page 96

Acorn Lap Throw, page 98

If the thought of sewing a full-size quilt seems a little intimidating to you, try your hand at a smaller project like this cozy appliquéd lap quilt. You'll soon be ready to take on larger projects!

"Listen! The wind is rising, and the air is wild with leaves. We have had our summer evenings, now for October eves!"

— Humbert Wolfe

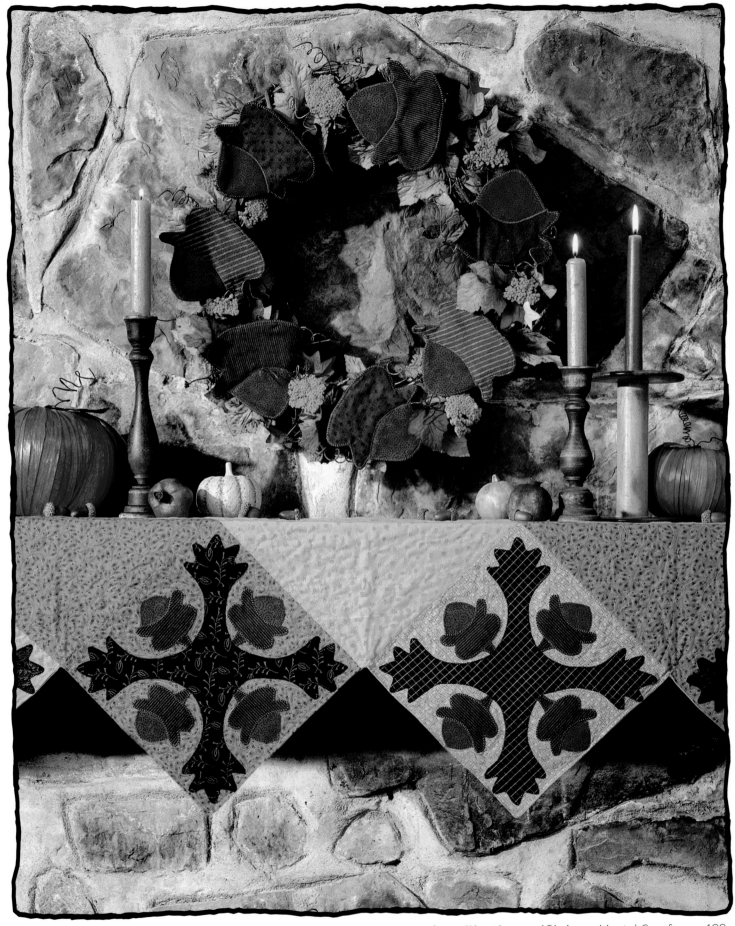

Acorn Wreath, page 101; Acorn Mantel Scarf, page 102

Acorn Block Pillow, page 103; Trip Around the World Pillow, page 104

*C*reate a cozy sitting area around the hearth…or even on the front porch! Toss comfy pillows on the chairs, drape a warm quilt over the couch and cover the mantel with a colorful scarf. Invite friends over to pop popcorn and play favorite board games…a great way to enjoy a chilly fall evening.

*O*ther items to arrange on your mantel for fall: beeswax candles, copper stars, bittersweet and a twig basket filled with pears, apples, gourds and mini pumpkins.

"Here's to October…frost-kissed apples, the wild-as-the-wind smell of hickory nuts and the nostalgic whiff of that first wood-smoke."

— Ken Weber

Around the World Table Mat, page 105

Remember coming home to a snack of milk & cookies? Make sweet memories with your own kids...greet them after school with acorn-shaped sugar cookies decorated with icing and sprinkles! You'll add a nostalgic feeling to the table when you make our scaled-down version of the Trip Around the World quilt pattern...it's just the right size for a colorful table mat.

Autumn leaves of russet, gold and red are pretty scattered down the center of the dining table...add a handful of acorns, too!

After-school SUGAR Cookies

7 T. BUTTER
⅓ C. SHORTENING
1 C. SUGAR
2 EGGS
1 t. VANILLA
2·½ C. ALL-PURPOSE FLOUR
1 t. BAKING POWDER
1 t. SALT

Cream together butter, shortening & sugar. Mix in eggs & vanilla ~ blend well. Mix in flour, baking powder & salt. Divide dough into two balls ~ wrap in plastic wrap. Chill a minimum of one hour. Roll dough out to ⅛" thickness on lightly-floured surface. Cut into desired shapes. Bake at 375 degrees for six to eight minutes on ungreased cookie sheet. Decorate with icing after baked & cooled. Makes about four dozen cookies.

yummy!

36

When you're not busy stitching, pack your quilting supplies in a pretty craft basket...a neat, attractive way to keep everything close at hand!

*"The trees are in their autumn beauty,
The woodland paths are dry,
Under the October twilight
The water mirrors a still sky."*

— William Butler Yeats

Craft Keeper, page 107

Friendship Gifts

The Country Friends® love to surprise each other with thoughtful handmade gifts! Kate and Mary Elizabeth know that Holly collects buttons, so they stitched up a pretty button basket wall hanging and pillow for her birthday. Wouldn't someone you know enjoy a treat like that? Turn the page for more neat gifts to make.

Button Wall Hanging, page 107

DETAILS, DETAILS!

When you're making button crafts, you may want to experiment using the buttons **with and without** thread in the holes. Please your eye ～ does it look better to have a snazzy shot of colored thread running through the design, or does the beauty of the button stand alone?

Beauty is in the eye of the beholder.
—OLD SAYING

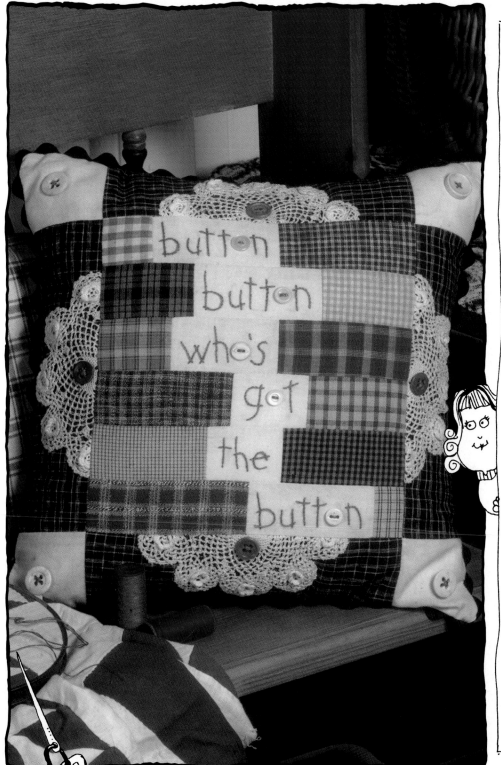

Button Pillow, page 109

In the late 1880's, young girls in the United States were crazy for "charm strings," long chains of buttons collected one by one and sewn together. The goal was to amass 1,000 buttons...it was said that Prince Charming would arrive after the 999th button was sewn on!

Liberty Pouch, page 109

Bee Project Keeper, page 111; Bee Needle Case, page 112

THE PLEDGE OF ALLEGIANCE

"I pledge allegiance to the flag of the United States of America and to the Republic for which it stands, one Nation under God, indivisible, with *Liberty* and *Justice* for all."

★ Public school children have been reciting that simple pledge since **1892.**

Add patriotic flair to a tiny purse with a homespun flag, or delight a crafty friend with the "bee-utiful" project pouch and needle case. Our simple wall hanging shares a loving sentiment.

Nothing is better than a Loyal friend.

~EURIPIDES

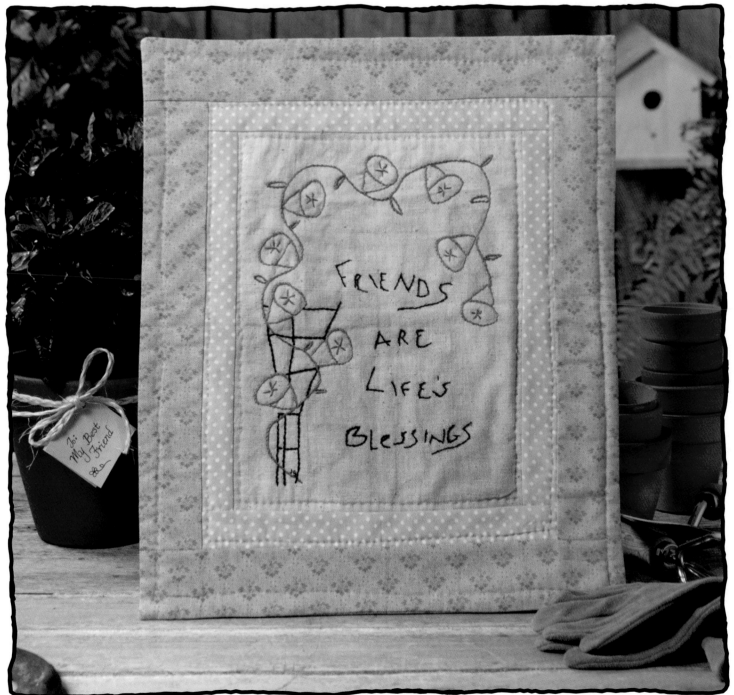

FRIENDS ARE LIFE'S BLESSINGS

"Friends" Wall Hanging, 113

ONE NATION WALL HANGING

(shown on pg. 4)

Finished Size: 23" x 32"

FABRICS

Yardage is based on 45"w fabric.
- cream print — ¼-yd
- red plaid — ¼-yd
- scraps of assorted cream prints for background
- scraps of assorted prints and plaids for appliqués and pieced squares
- fabric for backing and hanging sleeve — 1¼-yds
- fabric for binding — 1-yd

Other supplies
- batting — 45" x 60"
- heavy-duty paper-backed fusible web
- black permanent fabric marker

*Refer to **Assembly Diagram** and **Wall Hanging Top Diagram** as needed. See **Quilter's Basics** (pg. 115) for more in-depth basic instructions.*

CUTTING

Cream Print:
- Cut 1 strip 5¾"w. From this strip, cut: 5 squares 5¾" x 5¾", then cut each twice diagonally into 20 triangles.

Red Plaid:
- Cut 1 strip 5¾"w. From this strip, cut: 4 squares 5¾" x 5¾", then cut each twice diagonally into 16 triangles.
- Cut 2 squares 5⅜" x 5⅜", then cut each once diagonally into 4 corner triangles.

Cream Scraps:
- 1 A — 4½" x 9"
- 1 B — 4½" x 10"
- 1 C — 3" x 13½"
- 1 D — 5½" x 18½"
- 1 E — 3" x 8"
- 1 F — 3" x 11"
- 1 G — 5" x 7¼"
- 1 H — 5" x 11¾"
- 1 I — 3" x 18½"
- 1 J — 5¼" x 13½"
- 1 K — 5¼" x 5½"

Assorted Prints and Plaids:
- Cut 23 squares — 1¾" x 1¾".

Use patterns, pages 43 – 45, and follow **Preparing Appliqué Pieces**, page 119, to make the following appliqués.

- 5 stars
- 3 houses – 3" x 3⅜"
- 3 roofs
- 3 house sides
- 3 chimneys – ¾" x ¾"
- 3 doors – 1" x 2¼"
- 4 windows – 1" x 1"
- 1 tulip
- 1 tulip stem
- 1 violet
- 1 violet center
- 1 violet stem
- 1 sunflower
- 1 sunflower center
- 1 sunflower stem
- 1 flagpole – ½" x 11¾"

- 1 flag stars – 1⅞" x 2"
- 2 flag stripes – ½" x 3⅞"
- 2 flag stripes – ½" x 5¾"
- 3 tree trunks – ½" x ¾"
- 3 treetops
- 3 tree centers
- 3 tree bottoms
- 3 bodies
- 2 dresses
- 1 shirt
- 1 pants
- 1 boy hair piece
- 2 girl hair pieces
- 1 large heart
- 1 small heart

PIECING

1. Sew 8 squares together to make Unit 1. Sew 15 squares together to make Unit 2.

Unit 1 – make 1

Unit 2 – make 1

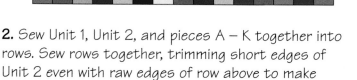

2. Sew Unit 1, Unit 2, and pieces A – K together into rows. Sew rows together, trimming short edges of Unit 2 even with raw edges of row above to make center section of wall hanging top.

3. Sew 7 triangles together to make Top/Bottom Border. Make 2 Top/Bottom Borders. Sew 11 triangles together to make Side Border. Make 2 Side Borders.

Top/Bottom Border - make 2

Side Border - make 2

4. Sew Top, Bottom, and Side Borders to center section. Sew 1 corner triangle to each corner of center section.

5. Follow manufacturer's instructions to fuse appliqués to center section to complete Wall Hanging Top.

6. Use permanent marker and dashed lines to write "One flag, one land, one heart, one hand," on wall hanging top. Write "One nation evermore!" on heart; write "Oliver Wendell Holmes" below heart.

FINISHING

1. Mark, layer, and quilt wall hanging, stitching in the ditch along seamlines.

2. Follow **Making a Hanging Sleeve**, pg. 126, to attach hanging sleeve to wall hanging.

3. Follow **Binding**, pg. 124, to bind wall hanging using 1³/₄"w straight-grain binding with mitered corners.

Wall Hanging Top Diagram

Assembly Diagram

Small Heart
Cut 1

Shirt
Cut 1

Star
Cut 5

Dress
Cut 2

Pants
Cut 1

Boy Hair Piece
Cut 1

Girl Hair Piece
Cut 2

Body
Cut 3

Large Heart
Cut 1

Tree Top
Cut 3

Tree Center
Cut 3

Tree Bottom
Cut 3

Roof
Cut 3

Tulip
Cut 1

Violet
Cut 1

Violet
Center
Cut 1

Tulip Stem
Cut 1

Violet Stem
Cut 1

House Side
Cut 3

Sunflower
Cut 1

Sunflower
Center
Cut 1

Sunflower Stem
Cut 1

45

PATRIOTIC QUILT

(shown on pg. 5)

Finished Size: 75½" x 89"
Block Size: 10" x 10"

FABRICS

Yardage is based on 45"w fabric.
- white for borders — 2¾-yds
- assorted white prints for squares and triangle-squares — 2½-yds total
- blue print for borders and sashing — 3¾-yds
- assorted blue prints for triangle-squares — 1¾-yds total
- red — 1⅛-yds
- fabric for backing and hanging sleeve — 5⅞-yds
- fabric for binding — 2¾-yds

Other supplies
- batting — 81" x 96"

Refer to **Quilt Top Diagram** as needed. See **Quilter's Basics** (pg. 115) for more in-depth basic instructions.

CUTTING

White:
- Cut 2 top/bottom middle borders 2¼" x 72".
- Cut 2 side middle borders 2¼" x 89".

Assorted White Print:
- Cut 8 strips 2¾"w. From this strip, cut: 120 squares 2¾" x 2¾".
- Cut 6 pieces 18" x 21" for triangle-squares.

Blue Print:
- Cut 2 top/bottom inside borders 2¼" x 68½".
- Cut 2 side inside borders 2¼" x 85½".
- Cut 2 top/bottom outside borders 2¼" x 75½".
- Cut 2 side outside borders 2¼" x 92½".
- Cut 4 long sashing strips 4" x 78".
- Cut 25 short sashing strips 4" x 10½".

Assorted Blue Print:
- Cut 6 pieces 18" x 21" for triangle-squares.

Red:
- Cut 2 strips 10½"w. From this strip, cut: 30 long sashing strips 1½" x 10½".
- Cut 3 strips 5"w. From this strip, cut: 60 short sashing strips 1½" x 5".

PIECING

1. To make triangle-squares, use assorted white print pieces and assorted blue print pieces and follow **Making Triangle-Squares** (pg. 117) to make 360 triangle-squares.

Fig. 1

triangle-square – make 360

2. Sew 3 triangle-squares and 1 square together to make Unit 1. Make 120 Unit 1's.

Unit 1 – make 120

3. Sew 2 Unit 1's and 1 short red sashing strip together to make Unit 2. Make 60 Unit 2's.

Unit 2 - make 60

4. Sew 2 Unit 2's and 1 long red sashing strip together to make Block. Make 30 Blocks.

Block - make 30

5. Sew 6 Blocks and 5 short blue sashing strips together to make Row. Make 5 Rows.

Row — make 5

6. Sew 5 rows and 4 long blue sashing strips together to make Quilt Top.

7. Follow **Adding Squared Borders**, pg. 121, to sew top, bottom, then side inside blue borders to quilt top. Sew middle white borders, then outside blue borders to quilt top in same manner.

FINISHING

1. Mark, layer, and quilt as desired. Our quilt is hand quilted in diagonal lines across the quilt top.

2. Follow **Binding**, pg. 124, to bind quilt using $9^{3}/_{8}$-yds of $2^{1}/_{2}$"w straight-grain binding with overlapping corners.

Quilt Top Diagram

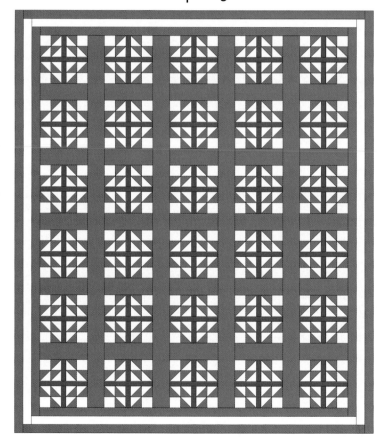

PATRIOTIC SHAMS

(shown on pg. 5)

Finished Size: 34" x 28" each

FABRICS FOR EACH SHAM
• white print — $1^{5}/_{8}$-yds
• blue striped print for trim — 1-yd
Other supplies
• white fleece — 1-yd
• fabric marking pen

CUTTING
White Print:
• Cut 1 front 35" x 29".
• Cut 2 back pieces 20" x 29".
Blue Striped Print:
We used a fabric that had a lengthwise design that created a striped effect. When cut, the design was centered in each strip.
• Centering design, cut 4 lengthwise strips $1^{1}/_{2}$"w for center trim. From these strips, cut:
  •2 top/bottom strips 27" long.
  •2 side strips 21" long.
• Centering design, cut 4 lengthwise strips $1^{1}/_{2}$"w for edge trim. From these strips, cut:
  •2 top/bottom strips 35" long.
  •2 side strips 29" long.
White Fleece:
• Cut 1 top backing 35" x 29".

INSTRUCTIONS
Use $1/_{2}$" seam allowances.

1. To make trim, press long edges of strips $1/_{4}$" to wrong side. Press ends $1/_{2}$" to wrong side.

2. Mark $4^{1}/_{2}$" from all edges of top. Matching outside edge of trim to mark and overlapping ends, topstitch center trim in place.

3. Matching raw edges, baste fleece to wrong side of front.

4. Press one long edge of each back piece $1/_{4}$" to wrong side; press $1/_{4}$" to wrong side again. Stitch along folded edge.

5. Sew backs to front, matching raw edges and right sides and overlapping back pieces.

6. Turn sham and press.

7. Matching outside edge of trim to edge of sham top and overlapping ends, topstitch edge trim in place.

Sham Diagram

34"
26"
28"
20"
3¼"

PIECING

1. Alternating fabrics, sew red and white print strips together to make pillow top.

2. Press 1 short side and 1 long side of blue rectangle ¼" to wrong side.

3. Follow manufacturer's instructions to fuse appliqué to blue rectangle. Follow **Invisible Appliqué**, pg. 119, to appliqué star.

4. Matching raw edges of blue rectangle to raw edges of pillow top, topstitch rectangle in place.

FINISHING

1. Matching right sides and raw edges, sew pillow top to pillow backing, leaving an opening for turning.

2. Stuff pillow with fiberfill; sew opening closed.

Pillow Top Diagram

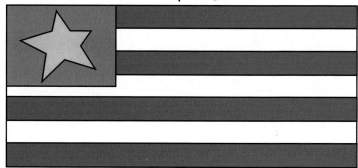

FLAG PILLOW

(shown on pg. 5)

Finished Size: 10½" x 21"

FABRICS

Yardage is based on 45"w fabric.
• 4 assorted red prints — scraps
• 3 assorted white prints — scraps
• blue print — scrap
• gold print — scrap
• fabric for backing — ⅜-yd

Other supplies
• polyester fiberfill
• paper-backed fusible web
• clear nylon thread

Refer to **Pillow Top Diagram** *as needed. See* **Quilter's Basics** *(pg. 115) for more in-depth basic instructions.*

CUTTING
Red Prints:
• From each fabric, cut 1 strip 2" x 21½".
Cream Prints:
• From each fabric, cut 1 strip 2" x 21½".
Blue Print:
• Cut 1 rectangle 5¾" x 9¼"
Gold Print:
• Use Star pattern, page 50, and follow **Preparing Appliqué Pieces**, page 119, to make the star appliqué.
Backing Fabric:
• Cut 1 rectangle 11" x 21½".

STAR PILLOW

(shown on pg. 6)

Finished Size: 14" square

FABRICS

Yardage is based on 45"w fabric.
• 12 assorted red and blue prints — scraps
• assorted tan prints for stars, borders, and insert — 1-yd total
• navy print for backing, lining, and ties — 1-yd

Other supplies
• polyester fiberfill
• paper-backed fusible web
• clear nylon thread

See **Quilter's Basics** *(pg. 115) for more in-depth basic instructions.*

CUTTING

Assorted red and blue prints:
- From each fabric, cut 1 rectangle 2½" x 6½".

Assorted Tan Prints:
- Use patterns, page 50, and follow **Preparing Appliqué Pieces**, page 119, to make star appliqués.
- For borders, cut 2 pieces 1⅞" x 12½".
- For pillow, cut 2 pieces 14½" x 14½".

Navy Print:
- For backing, cut 1 piece 12½" x 15¼".
- For lining, cut 1 piece 12½" x 30½".
- For ties, cut 8 pieces 1½" x 12".

PIECING

1. Sew 2 blue rectangles and 1 red rectangle together to make Unit 1. Make 2 Unit 1's.

Unit 1 – make 2

2. Sew 2 red rectangles and 1 blue rectangle together to make Unit 2. Make 2 Unit 2's.

Unit 2 – make 2

3. Sew 2 Unit 1's and 2 Unit 2's together to make Unit 3.

Unit 3

4. Sew 1 tan print border to top and bottom of Unit 3.

5. Follow manufacturer's instructions to fuse appliqués to Pillow Cover Top (Fig. 1). Follow **Invisible Appliqué**, pg. 119, to appliqué stars.

Fig. 1

6. Sew navy print backing piece to 1 border edge of Pillow Cover Top.

7. To make ties, press long edges of each tie piece ¼" to wrong side; press tie in half. Topstitch along folded edges. Refer to Fig. 2 to baste ties to pillow cover top (Note: Appliqués are not shown).

Fig. 2

4½"
6¼"
9"
6¼"

8. Press 1 short edge of pillow cover top and lining ¼" to wrong side. Matching right sides and raw edges and using a ¼" seam allowance, sew pillow cover top to lining along long edges. Turn and press.

9. With folded edges of cover overlapping raw edges of cover and forming a tube, whipstitch opening closed.

FINISHING

1. Follow **Pillow Finishing**, pg. 127, to make a knife-edge pillow.

2. Insert pillow in pillow cover; tie bows.

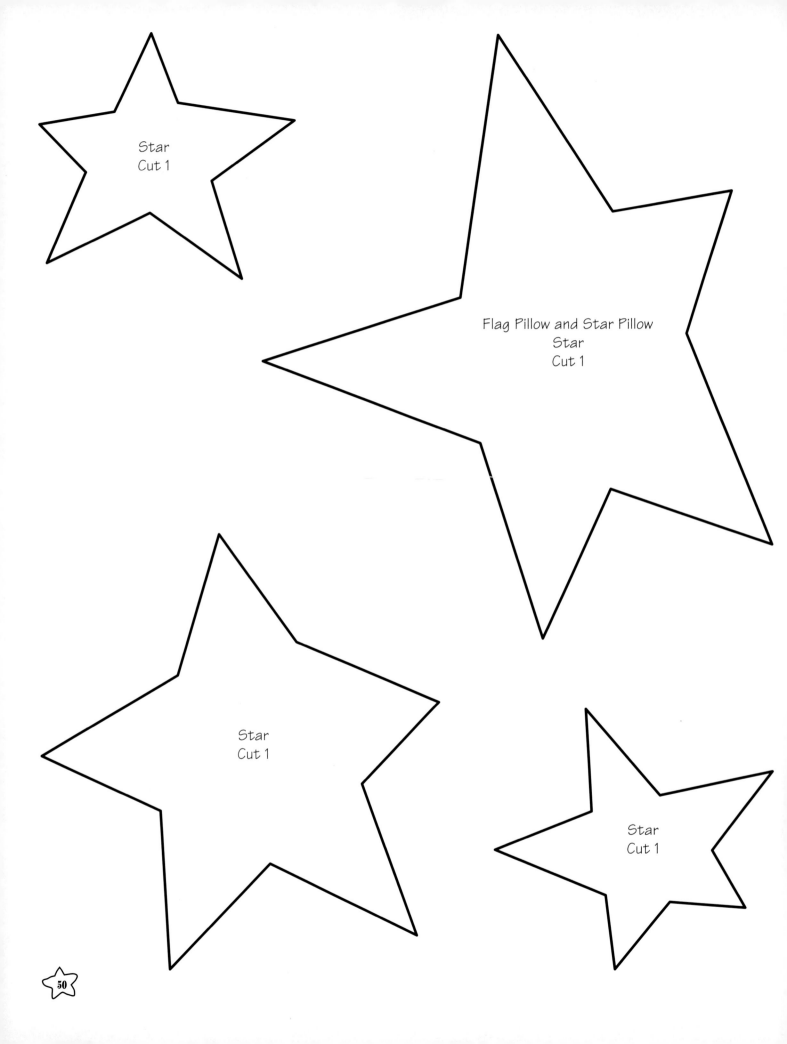

Star
Cut 1

Flag Pillow and Star Pillow
Star
Cut 1

Star
Cut 1

Star
Cut 1

DANCING STAR QUILT

(shown on pg. 7)

Finished Size: 50³/₄" x 60¹/₂"
Block Size: 12³/₄" x 12³/₄"

FABRICS

Yardage is based on 45"w fabric.
- assorted red, blue, and tan prints
- blue print for outer border — 1⁷/₈-yds
- fabric for backing — 3¹/₂-yds

Other supplies
- batting — 72" x 90"

Refer to **Quilt Top Diagram**, pg. 52, as needed. See **Quilter's Basics** (pg. 115) for more in-depth basic instructions.

CUTTING

Assorted red, blue, and tan prints:
- For each Star Block, cut:
  - 4 Strip A's — 2" x 10¹/₄".
  - 4 squares — 2" x 2".
- For each Fence Post Block, cut:
  - 12 rectangles — 2⁵/₈" x 6⁷/₈" (4 from each of 3 fabrics).
- For Borders, cut:
  - Strip B's — 1³/₄"w in random length for top/bottom inner borders.
  - Strip C's — 2¹/₄"w in random length for side inner borders.

Blue print:
- Cut 2 lengthwise strips 1³/₄" x 54³/₄" for top/bottom outer borders.
- Cut 2 lengthwise strips 1³/₄" x 64¹/₂" for side outer borders.

PIECING

1. Use patterns A-D (pgs. 53-54) and follow **Foundation Piecing** (pg. 118) to piece sections. Trim fabric and foundation ¹/₄" outside punched lines.

Unit 1

2. Sew 2 squares to each of 2 strips A's to make 2 Unit 2's.

Unit 2 – make 2

3. Sew Unit 1, 2 Strip A's, then 2 Unit 2's together to make Star Block. Repeat Steps 1-3 to make a total of 6 Star Blocks.

Star Block – make 6

4. Sew 3 rectangles together to make each of 4 Unit 3's.

Unit 3 – make 4

5. Sew 4 Unit 3's together to make Fence Post Block. Repeat Steps 5-6 to make a total of 6 Fence Post Blocks.

Fence Post Block – make 6

6. Sew 1 Star Block and 2 Fence Post Blocks together to make each of 2 Row A's.

Row A – make 2

7. Sew 2 Star Blocks and 1 Fence Post Block together to make each of 2 Row B's.

Row B – make 2

8. Sew rows together to make center section of quilt top.

9. Sew Strip B's together to make 6 long strips 1³/₄" x 38³/₄". Sew 3 long strips together to make top and bottom inner borders.

10. Sew Strip C's together to make 6 long strips 2¹/₄" x 59". Sew 3 long strips together to make 2 side inner borders.

11. Sew top, bottom, then side inner borders to center section of quilt.

12. Follow **Adding Mitered Borders**, pg. 122, to sew outer borders to quilt top using mitered corners.

Quilt Top Diagram

FINISHING

1. Layer backing (right side up), quilt top (right side down), then batting. Stitch all layers together ¹/₂" from outer edges leaving an opening for turning. Turn quilt right side out and slipstitch opening closed; press.

2. Mark and quilt as desired. Our quilt is hand quilted using an outline stitch.

DANCING STAR TABLE RUNNER

(shown on pg. 6)

Finished Size: 14³/₄" x 51"
Block Size: 12³/₄" x 12³/₄"

FABRICS

Yardage is based on 45"w fabric.
• assorted red, blue, and tan prints
• blue print for outer border and backing — 1⁵/₈-yds

Other supplies
• batting — 45" x 60"

*Refer to **Table Runner Top Diagram** as needed. See **Quilter's Basics** (pg. 115) for more in-depth basic instructions.*

PIECING

1. Follow Steps 1-5 of Dancing Star Quilt, pg. 51, to make 2 Star Blocks, 1 Fence Post Block, and 4 Unit 3's.

2. Sew 2 Unit 3's together to make each of 2 Half Fence Post Blocks.

Half Fence Post Block – make 2

3. Sew 2 Star blocks, 1 Fence Post Block, and 2 Half Fence Post Blocks together to complete center section of table runner top.

4. Cut 2 lengthwise strips 1³/₄" x 13¹/₄" and 2 lengthwise strips 1³/₄" x 54" for borders.

5. Sew borders to table runner top using mitered corners.

Table Runner Top Diagram

FINISHING

1. Layer backing (right side up), table runner top (right side down), then batting. Stitch all layers together ¹/₂" from outer edges leaving an opening for turning. Turn table runner right side out and slipstitch opening closed.

2. Mark and quilt as desired. Our table runner is hand quilted using an outline stitch.

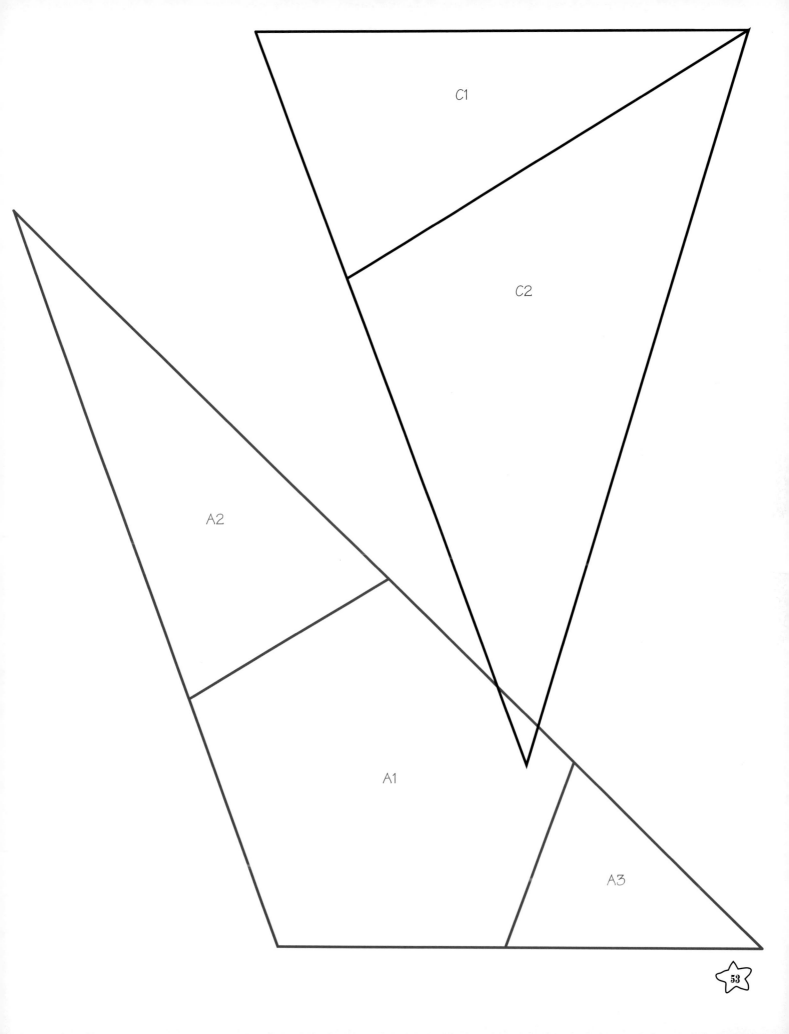

C1

C2

A2

A1

A3

53

"HOME SWEET HOME" WALL HANGING

(shown on pg. 8)

Finished Size: 23¹/₂" x 24"

FABRICS

Wool felt is available in 60"w or 72"w yardage and in 9" x 12" precut pieces.
- tan felt — ³/₄-yd
- dark red felt — ¹/₄-yd
- assorted colors for appliqués — 9" x 12" pieces
- scraps of wool plaid fabric for house appliqué

Other supplies
- assorted buttons
- embroidery floss to coordinate with felt colors
- water-soluble marker
- paper-backed fusible web
- tracing paper

*Refer to **Wall Hanging Top Diagram** as needed.*

CUTTING

Tan:
- Cut 2 pieces 23¹/₂" x 24" for top and back.
- Cut 1 hanging sleeve 3" x 24".

Dark Red:
- Cut 4 borders 1" x 24¹/₂".

Assorted Colors:
Use patterns, pgs. 57-58, and follow **Preparing Appliqué Pieces,** pg. 119, to make the following appliqués:

- 2 large flowers
- 2 large centers
- 8 medium flowers
- 8 medium centers
- 1 small flower
- 1 small flower center
- 1 small flower center circle
- 11 large leaves
- 5 medium leaves
- 2 small leaves
- 1 tree
- 1 rabbit
- 1 large star
- 1 small star
- 1 vase
- 1 vase trim
- 1 large triangle
- 4 small triangles
- 1 heart
- 1 zigzag heart
- 2 birds
- 2 wings
- 1 gable
- 2 windows ³/₄" x 1"
- 1 roof
- 1 background 6" x 7³/₄"
- 1 house end 1¹/₄" x 2¹/₂"
- 1 house front 2¹/₂" x 3¹/₄"

INSTRUCTIONS

Use 3 strands of floss for embroidery unless otherwise indicated.

1. Cut 4 strips of fusible web 1" x 24¹/₂". Trace Border pattern, pg. 57, onto paper side of each strip, repeating along length of strip. Follow manufacturer's instructions to fuse 1 web strip to one side of each border. Cut along scalloped line. Remove paper backing.

2. Fuse side, then top and bottom borders on wall hanging top 2" from outer edges. Trim ends of borders as needed.

3. Use water-soluble marker to draw a vertical line 5¹/₄" from straight edge of each side border and a horizontal line 6¹/₄" from straight edge of top border and bottom border.

4. Layer and arrange appliqués on wall hanging top; fuse in place. Trace words, "Home Sweet Home," pg. 57, onto tracing paper. Pin paper to area above house.

5. Follow **Hand Stitches**, pg. 127, to add embroidery details to appliqués and to work Running Stitch over marked lines, words, and for flower stems. Work Straight Stitches for birds' beaks. Do not add Cross Stitches to border at this time. Carefully tear away paper.

6. Matching wrong sides and raw edges, layer wall hanging top and back. Work Running Stitch along side and bottom edges. Pin hanging sleeve to back, matching top and side raw edges. Use a Running Stitch to sew all three layers together along top edge.

7. Use 6 strands of floss to work a Cross Stitch in the middle of each scallop on borders, catching bottom edge of hanging sleeve on top border.

8. Embellish with buttons as desired.

Wall Hanging Top Diagram

Stitch Diagram

"HOME SWEET HOME" FRAMED PIECE

(shown on pg. 9)

Finished Size: Fits a standard 9" x 12" frame.

FABRICS

Wool felt is available in 60"w or 72"w yardage and in 9" x 12" precut pieces.

- tan felt — 9" x 12" piece
- red felt — 9" x 12" piece
- green and gold felt for appliqués — scraps
- wool plaid fabric for house appliqué — scrap

Other supplies

- 9" x 12" frame
- 9" x 12" piece of adhesive mounting board
- 2 buttons
- embroidery floss — black, gold, and blue
- paper-backed fusible web
- hot glue gun and glue sticks
- tracing paper

CUTTING

Red:

- Cut 2 borders 1" x 12".
- Cut 2 borders 1" x 9".
- Cut 2 large flower centers.

Green:

- Cut 4 large leaves.
- Cut 2 trees.

Gold:

- Cut 2 large flowers.

Assorted Colors:

Referring to **Assembly Diagram,** use patterns, pgs. 57-58, and follow **Preparing Appliqué Pieces,** pg. 119, to make the following appliqués:

- 1 house front 2½" x 3¼"
- 1 roof
- 2 windows - ¾" x 1"
- 1 house end - 1¼" x 2½"
- 1 gable

INSTRUCTIONS

Use 3 strands of floss for embroidery unless otherwise indicated.

1. From paper-backed fusible web, cut two strips 1" x 9" and two strips 1" x 12". Trace Border pattern onto paper side of each strip, repeating along length of strip. Follow manufacturer's instructions to fuse 1 web strip to 1 side of each border. Cut along scalloped line. Remove paper backing.

2. Matching straight edges, fuse side, then top and bottom borders on tan felt.

3. Layer and arrange appliqués on tan felt piece; fuse in place. Trace words, "Home Sweet Home," onto tracing paper. Pin paper to area above house.

4. Follow **Hand Stitches**, pg. 127, to work Running Stitch over words. Carefully tear away paper. Work Running Stitch around trees, roof, and gable. Blanket Stitch around house front and house end. Use 6 strands of floss to work a Cross Stitch in the middle of each scallop on borders. Add embroidery details to leaves, flowers, and flower centers.

5. Adhere felt piece to sticky side of mounting board.

6. Mount felt piece in frame.

7. Place flower center on top of flower. Sew button to flower center through all layers. Glue leaves and flowers to corners of frame.

Assembly Diagram

Home Sweet Home

Medium Leaf

Small Flower

Medium Flower

Small Flower Center

Medium Center

Large Flower Center

Large Flower

Vase Trim

Large Leaf

Border

Small Flower Center Circle

Bird

Vase

Wing

Tree

Small Triangle

Large Triangle

Small Leaf

57

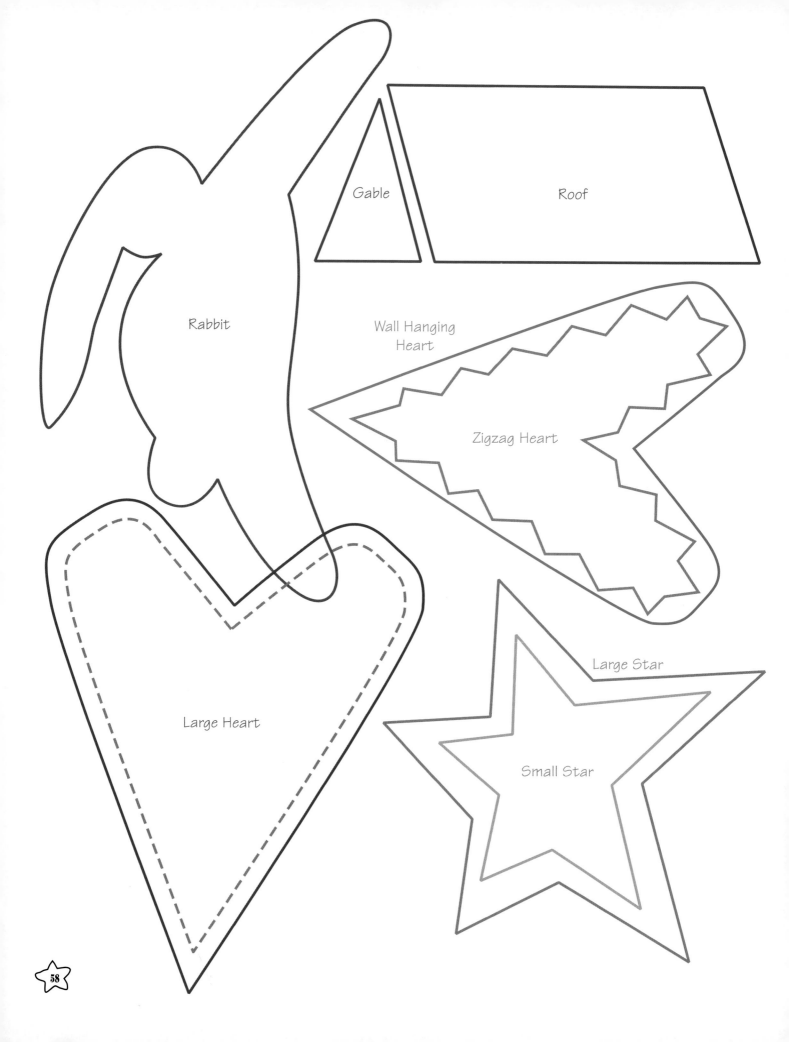

Gable

Roof

Rabbit

Wall Hanging
Heart

Zigzag Heart

Large Heart

Large Star

Small Star

58

STUFFED HEARTS

(shown on pg. 9)

Finished Size: Approximately $3^1/2$" x $4^1/2$"

SUPPLIES FOR EACH HEART

Wool felt is available in 60"w or 72"w yardage and in 9" x 12" precut pieces.
- green, gold, blue, red, and white felt — scraps
- embroidery floss — black
- thick, clear-drying craft glue
- polyester fiberfill

INSTRUCTIONS

Use 3 strands of floss for embroidery unless otherwise indicated.

1. Use patterns, pg. 57-58, to cut two Large Hearts, Zigzag Heart, Small Flower, Small Flower Center, Small Flower Center Circle, and 2 Small Leaves from desired colors.

2. Follow **Hand Stitches**, pg. 127, to Running Stitch $1/2$" from edge of one large heart and $1/4$" from edge of zigzag heart. Straight Stitch detail lines on leaves. Blanket Stitch around small flower. Use Cross Stitch to stitch small flower center circle to small flower center.

3. Matching right sides and raw edges, stitch large heart front to large heart back, leaving an opening for turning. Stuff with fiberfill.

4. Glue zigzag heart to large heart front, leaves and small flower to zigzag heart, and small flower center to small flower.

APPLE BUTTER JAR

(shown on pg. 10)

SUPPLIES

- glass jar with lid
- sheer fabric — $5^1/2$" square
- tag — $1^3/8$" x $2^3/4$"
- alphabet rubber stamps — $3/8$" tall
- black rubber stamp ink pad
- white string
- printed paper — slightly larger than tag
- craft glue

INSTRUCTIONS

1. Stamp "APPLE BUTTER" on tag. Glue tag to printed paper. Trim paper $1/4$" larger than tag on all sides. Attach string to tag.

2. Place sheer fabric over jar lid. Tie string around lid.

APPLE WALL HANGING

(shown on pg. 11)

Finished Size: $30^1/2$" x $30^1/2$"

FABRICS

Yardage is based on 45"w fabric.
- white — $1/2$-yd
- red print — $1/2$-yd
- variety of green prints to total $1/4$-yd
- brown print — $1/8$-yd
- green stripe — $5/8$-yd
- fabric for backing and hanging sleeve — $1^1/4$-yds
- fabric for binding — $5/8$-yd

Other supplies
- red jumbo rick rack — $12^1/2$-yds
- batting — 45" x 60"
- paper-backed fusible web

*Refer to **Wall Hanging Top Diagram**, pg. 60, as needed. See **Quilter's Basics** (pg. 115) for more in-depth basic instructions.*

CUTTING

White:
- Cut 2 strips 8"w. From these strips, cut:
  - 9 blocks 8" x 8".

Red Print:
- Use pattern, pg. 61, and follow **Preparing Appliqué Pieces**, pg. 119, to make 9 apple appliqués.

Green Print:
- Use pattern, pg. 61, to make 10 leaf appliqués.
- Cut 1 strip $2^1/2$"w. From this strip, cut:
  - 8 sashing squares $2^1/2$" x $2^1/2$".

Green Stripe:
- Cut 3 strips $2^1/2$"w. From these strips, cut:
  - 12 sashing strips $2^1/2$" x 8".
- Cut 4 strips $2^1/2$"w. From these strips, cut:
  - 4 border strips $2^1/2$" x 27".

Brown Print:
- Use pattern, page 61, to make 9 stem appliqués.

PIECING

1. Follow manufacturer's instructions to fuse appliqués to each white block.

2. Follow **Satin Stitch Appliqué**, pg. 120, to appliqué apples, leaves, and stems.

3. Cut 24 8" lengths of rick rack. Centering rick rack along $\frac{1}{4}$" seamline, baste rick rack to blocks as follows:

Block 1 – bottom and right side edges

Block 2 – bottom and side edges

Block 3 – bottom and left side edges

Block 4 – top, bottom, and right side edges

Block 5 – all sides

Block 6 – top, bottom, and left side edges

Block 7 – top and right side edges

Block 8 – top, left, and right side edges

Block 9 – top and left side edges

4. Sew Blocks 1, 2, and 3 and 2 sashing strips together to make Unit 1. Repeat with Blocks 4, 5, and 6 and Blocks 7, 8, and 9 to make 3 Unit 1's. Press seam allowances towards sashing strips.

Unit 1 – make 3

5. Sew 3 sashing strips and 2 sashing squares together to make Unit 2. Press seam allowances towards sashing strips. Make 2 Unit 2's.

Unit 2 – make 2

6. Sew Unit 1's and Unit 2's together to complete Unit 3.

Unit 3

7. Cut 4 27" lengths of rick rack. Centering rick rack along $\frac{1}{4}$" seamline, baste 1 length to each edge of Unit 3.

8. Sew 1 border strip to right and left sides of Unit 3.

9. Sew 1 sashing square to each end of remaining border strips. Sew border strips to top and bottom of Unit 3.

FINISHING

1. Mark, layer, and quilt wall hanging, outline quilting $\frac{1}{4}$" from edges of each appliqué; outline quilt $\frac{1}{4}$" from previous line of stitching. Quilt two diagonal lines across each sashing square to make an "X". Quilt a wavy line in each sashing strip and border strip.

2. Follow **Making a Hanging Sleeve**, pg. 126, to attach hanging sleeve to wall hanging.

3. Cut 4 31" lengths of rick rack. Centering rick rack along $\frac{1}{4}$" seamline, sew 1 length to each edge of wall hanging top.

4. Follow **Binding**, pg. 124, to bind wall hanging using a $19\frac{1}{2}$" square to make $2\frac{1}{2}$"w continuous bias binding with mitered corners.

Wall Hanging Top Diagram

SOFT-SCULPTURE APPLES

(shown on pg. 12)

Finished Size: Approximately 9" diameter

SUPPLIES FOR EACH APPLE

- red print — scraps
- green solid — scraps
- green embroidery floss
- polyester fiberfill
- cinnamon stick — about 2" long and 1/4" diameter

INSTRUCTIONS

Use 3 strands of floss for embroidery unless otherwise indicated.

1. Trace apple section pattern onto tracing paper; cut out.

2. Use pattern to cut 6 sections from red print fabric.

3. Matching side edges and leaving straight edges unstitched, sew 3 sections together to make a unit. Repeat with remaining sections. Sew the units together. Do not clip curves. Turn and stuff with fiberfill.

4. Fold straight edge of opening to inside of apple. Hand baste along folded edge, leaving long thread ends.

5. Refer to **Hand Stitches**, pg. 127, to stitch long Straight Stitches for veins in leaf.

6. Glue cinnamon stick into opening. Knot basting thread tightly around stick. Glue leaf to apple.

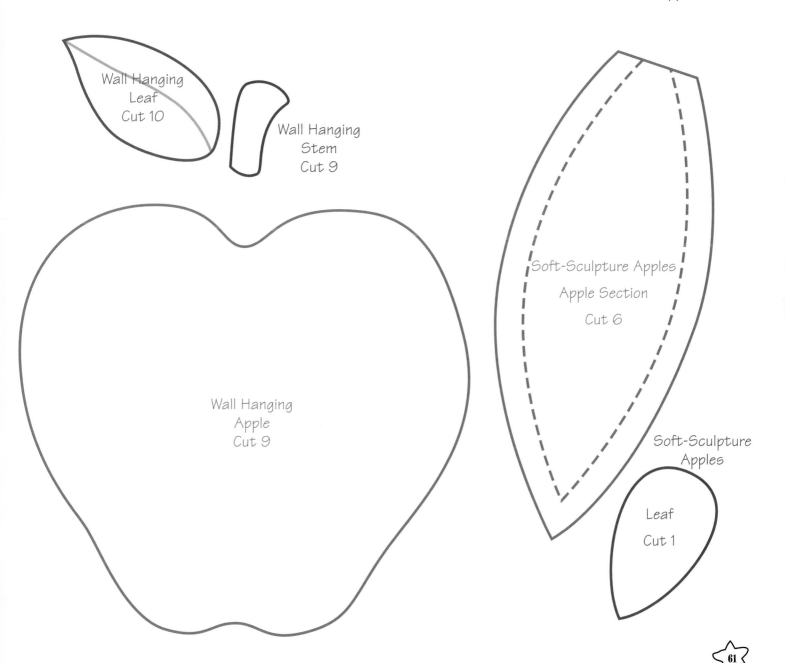

Wall Hanging Leaf Cut 10

Wall Hanging Stem Cut 9

Wall Hanging Apple Cut 9

Soft-Sculpture Apples Apple Section Cut 6

Soft-Sculpture Apples Leaf Cut 1

APPLE PLACE MAT AND NAPKIN

(shown on pg. 13)

Finished Size: 17" X 14½" with 14" square napkin

FABRICS FOR 1 PLACE MAT AND NAPKIN

Yardage is based on 45"w fabric.
• red solid — 1-yd
• green print — ½-yd
• scrap of brown print for stem
Other supplies
• fleece — 18" x 30"
• tracing paper

INSTRUCTIONS

1. Cut red solid fabric in two 18" x 15½" pieces. Place 1 piece right side down on a flat surface. Layer fleece, then remaining fabric piece on top, gently smoothing any wrinkles; pin layers together.

2. Spacing lines 1" apart, sew diagonal lines across the layered pieces. Repeat to stitch diagonal lines in the opposite direction across the layered pieces.

3. Trace patterns, pg. 63, onto tracing paper, matching dashed lines and turning paper as needed to make a complete half-pattern; cut out.

4. Use pattern to cut an apple shape from quilted fabric.

FINISHING

1. For loop, cut a 2" x 4½" piece of brown print fabric. Press each long edge ½" to wrong side; press piece in half lengthwise. Stitch together along folded edges. Matching raw edges, sew end of loop to top center of place mat front using a ⅜" seam allowance.

2. Follow **Binding**, pg. 124, to cut 1½-yds of 2½"w continuous bias binding. Sew binding to front of place mat. Matching raw edges, sew remaining end of loop to top center of place mat back using a ⅜" seam allowance. Folding binding over to back of place mat, blindstitch binding to back, taking care not to stitch through to front of place mat.

3. For napkin, cut a 15" square from green print fabric. To hem, press one edge ¼" to wrong side; press to wrong side again. Stitch along inside folded edge. Repeat for remaining edges.

APPLE BREAD CLOTH

(shown on pg. 14)

Finished Size: 19½" square

FABRICS

Yardage is based on 45"w fabric.
• red print — ⅝-yd
• scraps for apple and leaf

INSTRUCTIONS

1. Cut a 20" square of red print fabric.

2. For hem, press edges ¼" to wrong side; press ¼" to wrong side again. Stitch along inside folded edge.

3. Use patterns, below, and follow **Preparing Appliqué Pieces,** pg. 119, to make apple and leaf appliqués.

4. Follow manufacturer's instructions to fuse appliqués to corner of bread cloth.

5. Follow **Satin Stitch Appliquéing**, pg. 120, to appliqué apple and leaves. Machine satin stitch the stem.

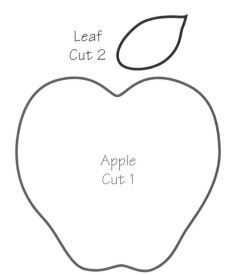

Leaf
Cut 2

Apple
Cut 1

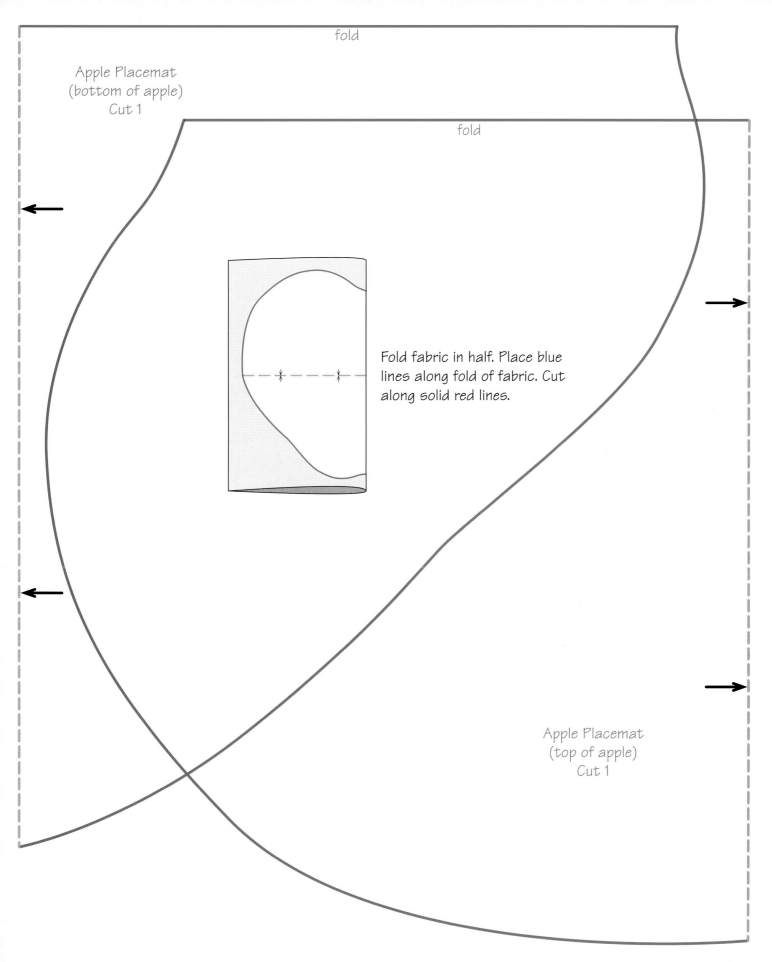

fold

Apple Placemat
(bottom of apple)
Cut 1

fold

Fold fabric in half. Place blue
lines along fold of fabric. Cut
along solid red lines.

Apple Placemat
(top of apple)
Cut 1

APPLIQUÉD APPLE HAND TOWELS

(shown on pg. 15)

Finished Size: 17" x 24"

FABRICS FOR 1 HAND TOWEL

Yardage is based on 45"w fabric.
• green stripe — ⁵/₈-yd
• scraps for apple, leaf, and stem

Other supplies
• jumbo rickrack — 17" length

INSTRUCTIONS

1. Cut a 17¹/₂" x 24¹/₂" piece of green stripe fabric.

2. Stitch length of rick rack 1¹/₂" above 1 short edge.

3. For hem, press edges ¹/₄" to wrong side; press ¹/₄" to wrong side again. Stitch along inside folded edge.

4. Use patterns, below, and follow **Preparing Appliqué Pieces,** pg. 119, to make apple, leaf, and stem appliqués.

5. Follow manufacturer's instructions to fuse appliqués to hand towel.

6. Follow **Satin Stitch Appliqué,** pg. 120, to appliqué apple, leaf, and stem.

Stem Cut 1

Leaf Cut 1

Apple Cut 1

CHEERY CHERRY WALL HANGING

(shown on pg. 16)

Finished Size: 33" x 33"

FABRICS

Yardage is based on 45"w fabric.
• white — ³/₈-yd
• pink stripe — ¹/₄-yd
• pink check — ¹/₄-yd
• blue polka-dot — ¹/₄-yd
• pink print — ¹/₄-yd
• blue plaid — ⁵/₈-yd
• green, dark green, and red fabrics for appliqués
• fabric for backing — 1¹/₄-yds
• fabric for binding — ¹/₂-yd

Other supplies
• batting — 45" x 60"
• paper-backed fusible web

Refer to **Wall Hanging Diagram,** *pg. 66, as needed.*
See **Quilter's Basics** *(pg. 115) for more in-depth basic instructions.*

CUTTING

White:
• Cut 4 squares 7¹/₂" x 7¹/₂".
• Cut 1 strip 3"w.

Pink Stripe:
• Cut 1 strip 2³/₄"w.

Pink Check:
• Cut 1 strip 2³/₄"w.

Blue Polka-dot:
• Cut 2 strips 2³/₄"w.
• Cut 1 strip 3"w.

Pink Print:
• Cut 4 strips 1³/₄"w. From these strips cut:
  • 2 strips 1³/₄" x 21¹/₂".
  • 2 strips 1³/₄" x 24".

Blue Plaid:
• Cut 4 strips 5"w. From these strips cut:
  • 2 strips 5" x 24".
  • 2 strips 5" x 33".

Green, dark green, and red:
• Use patterns, pg. 66, and follow **Preparing Appliqué Pieces,** pg. 119, to make the following appliqués:
  • 8 cherries.
  • 4 cherry stems.
  • 8 leaves.

PIECING

1. Follow manufacturer's instructions to fuse appliqués to white squares.

2. Follow **Satin Stitch Appliqué**, pg. 120, to appliqué cherries, stems, and leaves.

3. To make 9-patch blocks, sew pink stripe strip, 3"w blue polka-dot strip, and pink check strip together to make Strip Set A. Cut 10 2³/₄"w Unit 1's from strip set. Repeat with remaining polka dot strips and white strip to make Strip Set B and cut 5 3"w Unit 2's.

Strip Set A

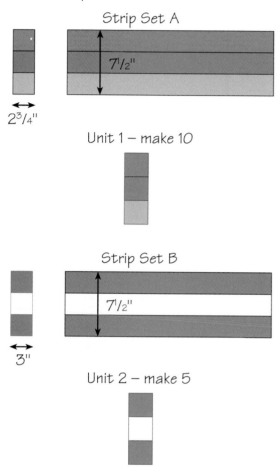

2³/₄"

Unit 1 — make 10

Strip Set B

3"

Unit 2 — make 5

4. Sew 2 Unit 1's and 1 Unit 2 together to make 5 9-patch blocks.

5. Sew 2 9-patch blocks and 1 appliquéd square together to complete Unit 3. Make 2 Unit 3's.

Unit 3 — make 2

6. Sew 2 appliquéd squares and 1 9-patch block together to complete Unit 4.

Unit 4

7. Sew Units 3 and 4 together to make Unit 5.

Unit 5

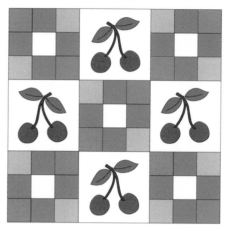

8. Sew pink print strips to sides, then top and bottom of background.

9. Sew plaid strips to sides, then top and bottom of background.

FINISHING

1. Mark, layer, and quilt. Quilt in the ditch on each side of the pink border. Outline quilt ¹/₈" from edges of cherry clusters. Echo quilt twice around each cherry cluster ¹/₄" apart. Quilt an "X" across each blue polka-dot square in each 9-patch block. Quilt motifs in remaining squares in each 9-patch block. Beginning in center, place curved edge of scallop pattern, pg. 66, along raw edge of border and mark scalloped cutting line along border. Echo quilt marked line 1" apart twice along border.

2. Trim along marked line.

3. Follow **Making Continuous Bias Strip Binding**, pg. 124, and use a 16" square of binding fabric to make 6¹/₂-yds of 1¹/₄"w continuous bias binding. Press one raw edge of binding ¹/₄" to wrong side. Match remaining raw edge to raw edge of quilt top and sew binding around quilt. To sew around scallops, pin binding to one scallop at a time as you sew. Gently ease binding around outer curves, being careful not to stretch it. At junctions between scallops, raise presser foot to turn the corner, keeping the fabric as smooth as possible. Trim batting and backing even with quilt top. Blindstitch binding to quilt backing.

Wall Hanging Diagram

Wall Hanging
Scallop

Leaf

Quilting
Pattern

Quilting
Pattern

Cherry
Stem

Wall Hanging
Scallop Corner

Cherry

66

CHEERY CHERRY CRIB QUILT

(shown on pg. 17)

Finished Size: 39¹/₂" x 47¹/₂"

FABRICS

Yardage is based on 45"w fabric.
- white — 1-yd
- pink print — ³/₈-yd
- blue plaid — 1-yd
- green, dark green, and red fabrics for appliqués
- fabric for backing and hanging sleeve — 1¹/₂-yds
- fabric for binding — ¹/₂-yd

Other supplies
- batting — 45" x 60"
- paper-backed fusible web
- embroidery floss — blue
- hot iron transfer pencil
- tracing paper

*Refer to **Quilt Top Diagram** as needed. See **Quilter's Basics** (pg. 115) for more in-depth basic instructions.*

CUTTING
White:
- For background, cut 1 rectangle 23" x 31".

Pink Print:
- Cut 4 strips 1³/₄"w. From these strips cut:
  - 2 strips 1³/₄" x 31".
  - 2 strips 1³/₄" x 25¹/₂".

Blue Plaid:
- Cut 4 strips 7¹/₂"w. From these strips cut:
  - 2 strips 7¹/₂" x 33¹/₂".
  - 2 strips 7¹/₂" x 39¹/₂".

Green, dark green, and red:
- Use patterns, pg. 66, and follow **Preparing Appliqué Pieces**, pg. 119, to make the following appliqués:
  - 14 cherries.
  - 7 cherry stems.
  - 10 leaves.

PIECING

1. Follow manufacturer's instructions to fuse appliqués to background.

2. Follow **Satin Stitch Appliqué**, pg. 120, to appliqué cherries, stems, and leaves.

3. Following manufacturer's instructions, use hot iron transfer pencil and patterns, pg. 68, to transfer verse to background. Refer to **Hand Stitches**, pg. 127, to Stem Stitch verse.

4. Sew pink print strips to sides, then top and bottom of background.

5. Sew plaid strips to sides, then top and bottom of background.

FINISHING

1. Mark, layer, and quilt. Quilt in the ditch on each side of the pink border. Outline quilt ¹/₈" from edges of cherry clusters. Echo quilt around each cherry cluster ¹/₄" apart. Beginning in center, place curved edge of scallop patterns, pg. 69, along raw edge of border and mark scalloped cutting line along border. Echo quilt marked line 1" apart twice.

2. Trim along marked line.

3. Follow **Making Continuous Bias Strip Binding**, pg. 124, and use an 18" square of binding fabric to make 7¹/₂-yds of 1¹/₄"w continuous bias binding. Press one raw edge of binding ¹/₄" to wrong side. Match remaining raw edge to raw edge of quilt top and sew binding around quilt. To sew around scallops, pin binding to one scallop at a time as you sew. Gently ease binding around outer curves, being careful not to stretch it. At junctions between scallops, raise presser foot to turn the corner, keeping the fabric as smooth as possible. Trim backing and batting even with edges of quilt top. Blindstitch back of binding to quilt backing.

Quilt Top Diagram

cheery

cherry

baby

looking

sweet

berry for ripe

Merry

A

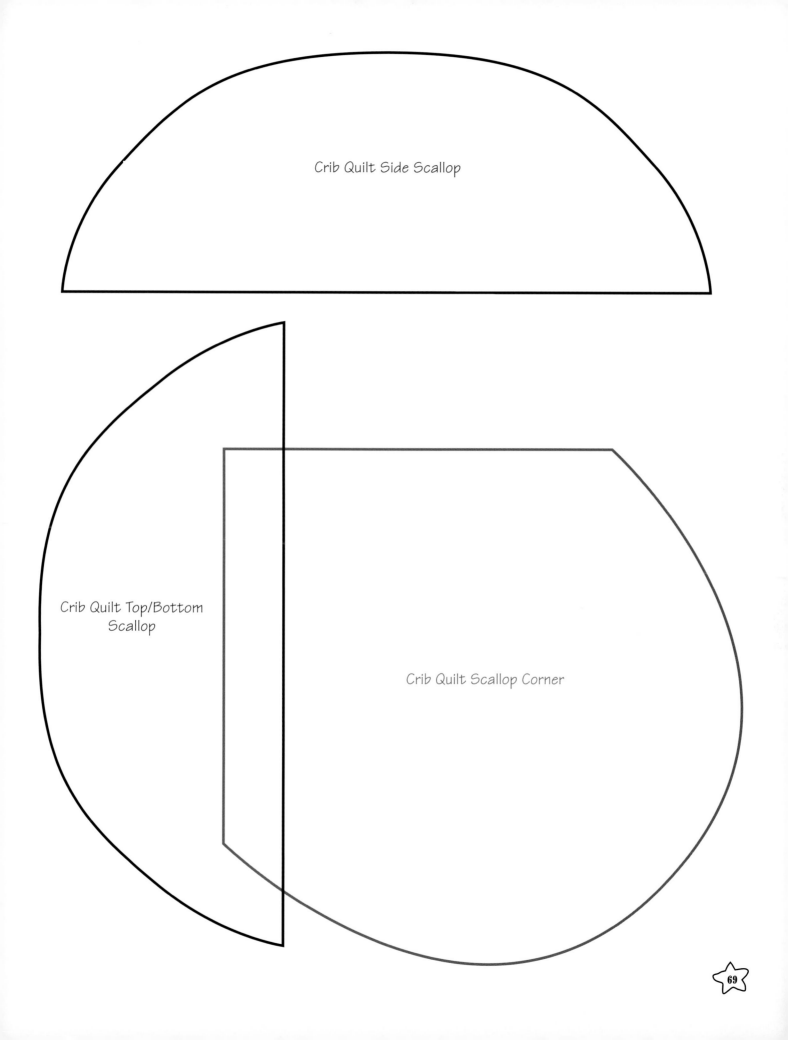

Crib Quilt Side Scallop

Crib Quilt Top/Bottom
Scallop

Crib Quilt Scallop Corner

BUMPER PADS
(shown on pg. 17)

Finished Size: Our bumper pads fit a standard
(27" x 52") baby crib.

FABRICS

Yardage is based on 45"w fabric.
- white — 2¹/₂-yds
- blue print — 2¹/₂-yds
- green, dark green, and red fabrics for appliqués

Other supplies
- 72"w upholstery batting — 2¹/₂-yds
- paper-backed fusible web

CUTTING
White:
- For panels, cut 4 rectangles 8" x 80".

Blue Print:
- Cut 8 lengthwise strips 2¹/₂"w. From these strips cut:
  - 8 strips 2¹/₂" x 80".
- For ties, cut 16 strips 2" x 16".

Green, dark green, and red:
- Use patterns, pg. 66, and follow **Preparing Appliqué Pieces**, pg. 119, to make the following appliqués:
  - 64 cherries.
  - 32 cherry stems.
  - 64 leaves.

Batting:
- Cut 2 rectangles 12" x 80".

PIECING
1. Sew 1 strip each to top and bottom edges of each panel.

2. Fuse 8 clusters of cherries to each panel. Follow **Satin Stitch Appliqué**, pg. 120, to appliqué cherries, stems, and leaves.

3. For ties, press each edge of strip ¹/₄" to wrong side; press strip in half lengthwise. Stitch along long edges. Fold each tie in half.

4. Referring to Fig. 1 (appliqués are not shown), mark each long edge of 2 Panels 26¹/₂" from ends. Lightly draw a line between marks across width of panel. Baste folded ends of ties as shown, adjusting location of ties at marks to fit the bed if necessary.

Fig. 1

5. Matching right sides and raw edges, place 1 panel with ties together with 1 panel without ties. Place 1 batting rectangle on top of panels; pin all layers together. Using a ¹/₂" seam allowance and sewing through all layers, sew panels together, leaving an opening for turning. Trim corners and turn right side out. Whipstitch opening closed.

6. Stitch across width of bumper panels (through all layers) along lines marked in Step 4.

7. Repeat Steps 3-6 to complete remaining pad.

CHAIR PAD
(shown on pg. 18)

Finished Size: 14" x 25"

FABRICS

Yardage is based on 45"w fabric.
- white — ¹/₄-yd
- pink stripe — ¹/₄-yd
- pink check — ¹/₄-yd
- blue polka-dot — ¹/₄-yd
- blue plaid — ¹/₄-yd
- green, dark green, and red fabrics for appliqués
- fabric for backing and ties — ³/₄-yd
- fabric for binding — ¹/₂-yd

Other supplies
- 72"w upholstery batting — ¹/₂-yd
- paper-backed fusible web

Refer to **Chair Pad Top Diagram** as needed. See **Quilter's Basics** (pg. 115) for more in-depth basic instructions.

CUTTING

White:
• Cut square 8" x 8".

Pink Stripe:
• Cut 1 strip 3"w. From this strip, cut:
  •4 rectangles 3" x 3½".

Pink Check:
• Cut 1 strip 3"w. From this strip, cut:
  •4 rectangles 3" x 3½".

Blue Polka-dot:
• Cut 1 strip 3½"w. From this strip, cut:
  •4 squares 3½" x 3½".
• Cut 1 strip 3"w. From this strip, cut:
  •4 rectangles 3" x 3½".

Blue Plaid:
• Cut 1 strip 6"w. From this strip cut:
  •2 rectangles 6" x 14".
• For ties, cut 2 strips 2" x 16".

Green, dark green, and red:
• Use patterns, pg. 66, and follow **Preparing Appliqué Pieces**, pg. 119, to make the following appliqués:
  •2 cherries.
  •1 cherry stem.
  •2 leaves.

PIECING

1. Follow manufacturer's instructions to fuse appliqués to white square.

2. Follow **Satin Stitch Appliqué**, pg. 120, to appliqué cherries, stem, and leaves.

3. Beginning and ending with a square, sew 2 polka-dot squares, 1 pink checked rectangle, 1 polka-dot rectangle, and 1 pink striped rectangle together to make Unit 1. Make 2 Unit 1's. Sew 1 pink checked rectangle, 1 blue polka-dot rectangle, and 1 pink striped rectangle together to make Unit 2. Make 2 Unit 2's.

Unit 1 – make 2

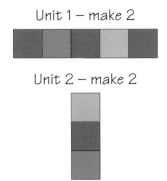

Unit 2 – make 2

4. Sew Unit 2's to each side of appliquéd block to make Unit 3.

Unit 3

5. Sew Unit 1's to Unit 3 to make Unit 4.

Unit 4

6. Sew borders to top and bottom of Unit 4.

FINISHING

1. Mark, layer, and quilt. Outline quilt ⅛" from edges of cherry clusters. Echo quilt twice around each cherry cluster ¼" apart. Quilt in the ditch around appliquéd block. Quilt an "X" across each small square. Quilt straight lines 2" apart on top and bottom borders.

2. For ties, press each edge of strip ¼" to wrong side; press strip in half lengthwise. Stitch along long edges. Fold each tie in half.

3. Referring to **Chair Pad Top Diagram**, baste folded ends of ties to back of chair pad.

4. Refer to **Binding**, pg. 124, to bind wall hanging using a 14" square of binding fabric to make 2¼-yds of 2½"w continuous bias binding with mitered corners.

Chair Pad Top Diagram

CHEERY CHERRY CHANGING PAD COVER

(shown on pg. 19)

Block Size: 10" x 10"

FABRICS

Yardage is based on 45"w fabric.
- white — ⅛-yd
- pink stripe — ⅛-yd **each**
- pink check — ⅛-yd
- blue polka-dot — ⅛-yd
- blue check print for borders, sashing, and backing — 1-yd

Other supplies
- changing pad
- safety pins

*See **Quilter's Basics** (pg. 115) for more in-depth basic instructions.*

CUTTING

White:
- Cut 2 squares $3^7/8$" x $3^7/8$".

Pink Prints:
- From each pink print, cut 1 strip $3^7/8$"w. From each strip, cut:
  - 4 squares $3^7/8$" x $3^7/8$".

Blue Polka-dot:
- Cut 1 strip $3^7/8$"w. From this strip, cut:
  - 8 squares $3^7/8$" x $3^7/8$".

Blue Check Print:
- Cut 1 sashing strip 3" x $10^5/8$".
- Cut 2 end borders $10^5/8$" x 12".

PIECING

1. Sew 2 pink print squares to 1 blue polka-dot square to make Unit 1. Make 4 Unit 1's.

Unit 1 – make 4

2. Sew 2 blue polka-dot squares to 1 white square to make Unit 2. Make 2 Unit 2's.

Unit 2 – make 2

3. Sew 2 Unit 1's and 1 Unit 2 together to make Block. Make 2 Blocks.

Block – make 2

4. Sew 2 end borders, 2 blocks, and 1 sashing strip together to make Unit 3.

Unit 3

5. Measure width and length of changing pad. **To determine width of side border strip**, subtract $10^5/8$" from width of changing pad. **To determine length of side border strip**, add 12" to length of changing pad. Cut 2 side border strips the determined measurements. Sew side borders to Unit 3.

6. Cut backing same size as changing pad cover top. Matching right sides and raw edges, sew top to backing along long sides to form a tube; turn.

7. To hem each end, press raw edge ¼" to wrong side; press to wrong side again. Sew along folded edges.

8. Place changing pad in tube. Fold ends to back and pin.

SNOWMAN WALL HANGING

(shown on pg. 22)

Finished Size: 21" x 21½"

FABRICS

Yardage is based on 45"w fabric.
- blue print — 1¼-yd
- red print — ¼-yd
- assorted fabrics for appliqués
- fabric for binding — ½-yd

Other supplies
- batting — 45" x 60"
- paper-backed fusible web
- embroidery floss — white and black
- 2 black buttons — ³⁄₁₆" diameter
- 3 black buttons — ¼" diameter
- white medium rickrack — 4 12³⁄₄" lengths
- hot iron transfer pencil
- tracing paper

Refer to **Wall Hanging Top Diagram** *as needed. See* **Quilter's Basics** *(pg. 115) for more in-depth basic instructions.*

CUTTING
Blue Print:
- For background, cut 1 rectangle 14" x 14½".
- For borders, cut 2 strips 3³⁄₄"w. From these strips, cut:
  - 2 top/bottom strips 3³⁄₄" x 14".
  - 2 side strips 3³⁄₄" x 21".
- For backing, cut 1 square 24" x 24".
- For hanging sleeve, cut 1 rectangle 4" x 20½".

Red Print:
- For trim, cut 2 strips 1¼"w.

Assorted Fabrics for Appliqués:
- Use patterns, pg. 76, and follow **Preparing Appliqué Pieces**, pg. 119, to make the following appliqués:

  - snowman head
  - snowman body
  - nose
  - cap
  - cuff
  - pom-pom
  - scarf
  - snow
  - star

PIECING

1. Follow manufacturer's instructions to fuse appliqués to background.

2. Follow **Satin Stitch Appliqué**, pg. 120, to appliqué snow, snowman body, snowman head, nose, scarf, cap, cuff, pom-pom, and star.

3. Sew blue print borders to top and bottom, then sides of background.

4. Sew trim strips together end to end. Press each long edge of trim ¼" to wrong side. Lay trim on background along border seamlines, mitering corners and overlapping ends. Fold end to wrong side. Lay lengths of rickrack under inside edge of trim; pin in place. Topstitch trim and rickrack in place.

5. Follow manufacturer's instructions and use hot iron transfer pencil to transfer words, pg. 79, and snowflake, pg. 76, to wall hanging top. Refer to **Hand Stitches**, pg. 127, to Backstitch words and snowflakes. Stitch white French Knots on ends of snowflake spokes. Stitch black French Knots for snowman's mouth. Sew buttons to snowman.

FINISHING

1. Mark, layer, and quilt. Hand quilt ⅛" outside appliqués. Quilt in the ditch along outside edge of trim. Refer to **Hand Stitches** to randomly stitch white French Knots on wall hanging top.

2. Follow **Making a Hanging Sleeve**, pg. 126, to attach hanging sleeve to wall hanging.

3. Follow **Binding**, pg. 124, to bind wall hanging using a 15" square of binding fabric to make 2⅝-yds of 2½"w continuous bias binding.

Wall Hanging Top Diagram

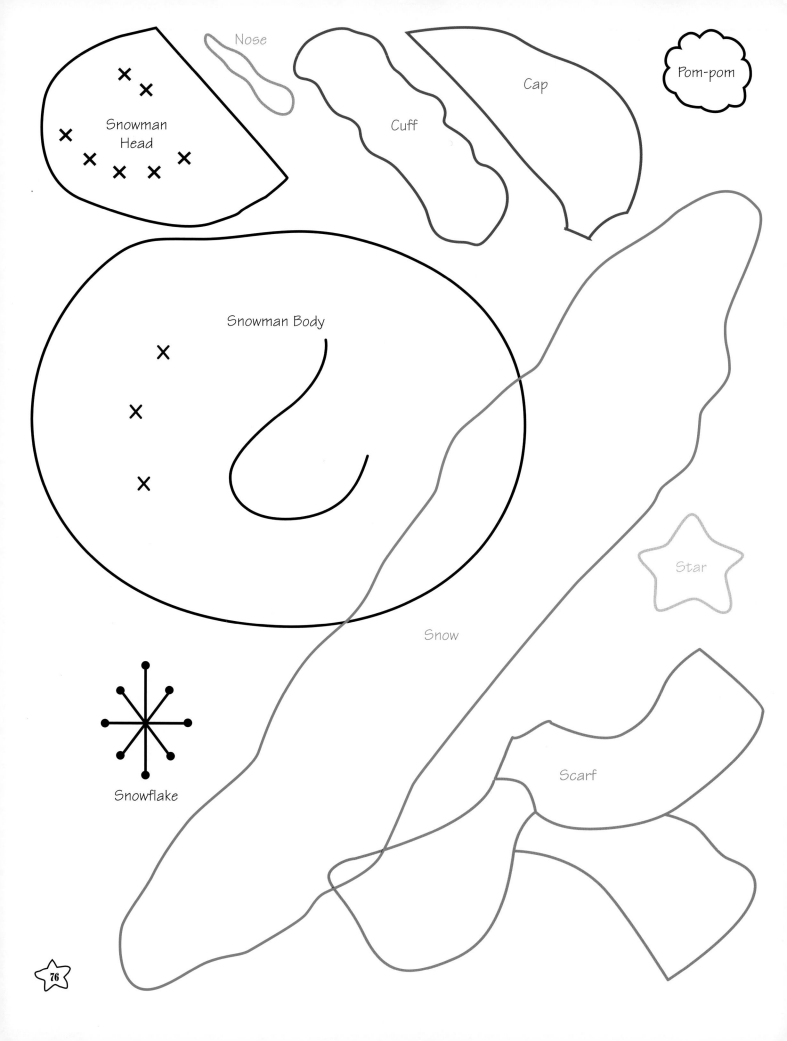

Nose

Cuff

Cap

Pom-pom

Snowman
Head

Snowman Body

Star

Snow

Snowflake

Scarf

76

CHENILLE SNOWMAN

(shown on pg. 23)

Finished Size: Approximately 14" tall

FABRICS

Yardage is based on 45"w fabric.
- white chenille — $1/2$-yd
- green fleece — $1/2$-yd
- green stripe — scrap
- red print — $1/4$-yd
- white felt — $1/4$-yd
- orange felt — scrap
- 3 assorted fabrics for stars — scraps

Other supplies
- polyester fiberfill
- paper-backed fusible web — $1/4$-yd
- yellow paint
- paintbrush
- embroidery floss — red
- wooden stars — 1 $2^3/4$"w and 2 2"w
- black buttons — 2 $7/16$" dia., 3 $5/8$" dia., and 5 $5/16$" dia.
- white buttons — 1 $3/4$" diameter and 2 $9/16$" diameter
- white medium rickrack — 2 $2^1/2$" lengths
- red jumbo rickrack — 14" length
- red baby rickrack — 5" length
- green satin ribbon — 40" length
- orange thread for nose
- white floss for tassel — two 8" lengths
- fabric glue

CUTTING

White Chenille:
- Use patterns, pgs. 78-79, to cut 2 snowman bodies and 4 arms.

Green Fleece:
- Cut a 14" square.

Green Stripe:
- Cut a 3" x 14" piece.
- Follow manufacturer's instructions to fuse paper-backed fusible web to wrong side of fabric. Cut a $4^1/4$" x $2^1/2$" piece.

White Felt:
- Cut a $34^1/2$" x 5" piece.

Orange Felt:
- Use pattern, pg. 78, to cut nose.

Match right sides and raw edges and use a $1/4$" seam allowance for all sewing.

INSTRUCTIONS

1. Sew 2 arm pieces together leaving straight edge open; turn. Stuff arm with fiberfill. Repeat for remaining arm pieces.

2. With arms facing in, baste arms to 1 body piece.

3. Sew $7/16$" buttons to one body piece for eyes. Sew $5/16$" buttons to body piece for mouth. Sew $5/8$" buttons to body. Sew body front to body back, leaving an opening for turning; turn. Stuff body with fiberfill. Sew opening closed.

4. For nose, start at one straight side and roll into nose shape. Sew final side closed. Wrap thread around nose; secure. Sew wide end of nose to face. Folding nose to one side, secure nose to face.

5. For cap, fold 14" square of fleece in half. Measure over 3" from top right corner; mark. Draw a line from mark to lower right hand corner. Sew along drawn line; trim $1/4$" from stitching.

6. For cuff, sew short ends of 3" x 14" green stripe piece together. Fold cuff in half lengthwise. Matching raw edges of cuff to wrong side of cap, sew cuff to cap. Fold cuff to outside. Referring to **Hand Stitches**, pg. 127, and overlapping ends at seam, use floss to sew jumbo rick rack to cuff with a Running Stitch.

7. For tassel, cut white felt into $1/2$" x 5" pieces. Lay 1 floss length on flat surface. With strips of white felt perpendicular to floss length, stack strips on top of each other. Knot floss ends around center of strips. Smoothing strips, tie remaining floss length around top of tassel. Glue baby rick rack around top of tassel. Gather open end of cap. Glue tassel to cap over gathers.

8. For scarf, cut 2 pieces $2^3/8$" x $27^1/2$". Holding all ends together, trim ends at a diagonal. Cut $2^1/2$" x $4^1/4$" piece of green stripe fabric into thin strips approx. $1/8$"w. Fuse strips and glue white rick rack in parallel lines on each end of 1 scarf piece. Matching right sides and raw edges, sew scarf pieces together, leaving an opening for turning; turn. Sew opening closed.

9. For star garland, paint stars yellow. Draw around wooden stars on paper side of fusible web. Fuse web to wrong sides of star fabrics. Cut out along drawn lines. Fuse fabric stars to wooden stars. Sew through remaining buttons with yellow thread. Hot glue buttons to stars. Cut green ribbon into 1 20" length and 2 10" lengths. Knot short lengths around long length approx. 5" from ends. Hot glue knots to snowman's hands. Fold ends of ribbons in half lengthwise and trim diagonally to form "V."

Nose
Cut 1

Arm
Cut 4

Snowman Body
Cut 2

Place on fold of fabric.

Aligning grey dashed lines and arrows, trace pattern onto tracing paper. Fold fabric in half. Place blue lines along fold of fabric. Cut along solid black line.

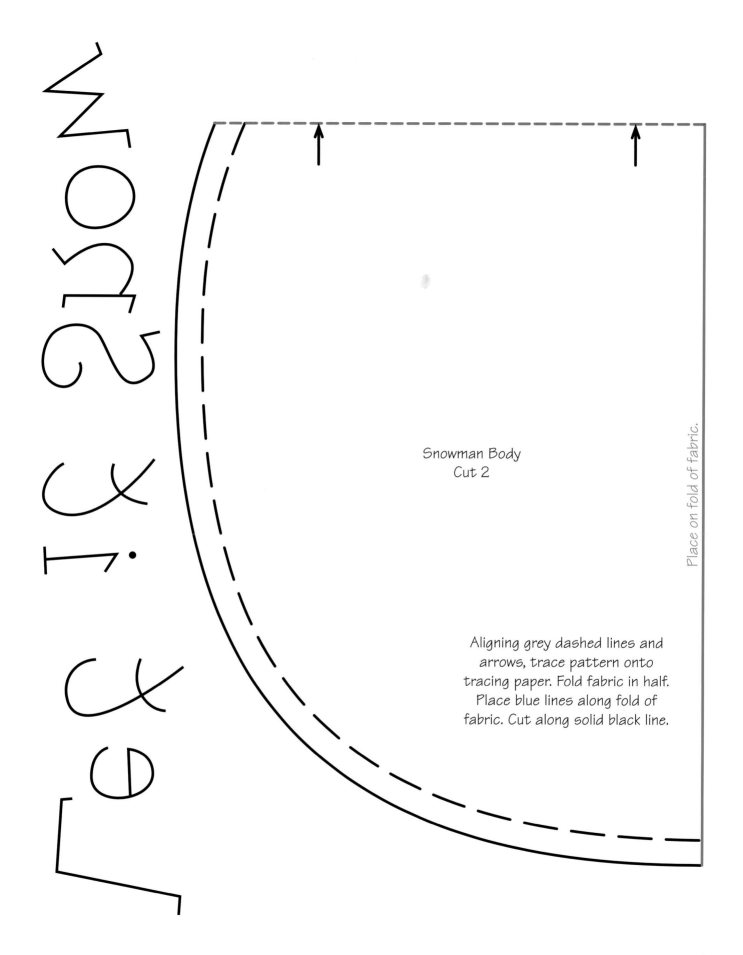

Snowman Body
Cut 2

Place on fold of fabric.

Aligning grey dashed lines and
arrows, trace pattern onto
tracing paper. Fold fabric in half.
Place blue lines along fold of
fabric. Cut along solid black line.

SNOWMAN PILLOW

(shown on pg. 23)

Finished Size: 14" square excluding flange

FABRICS

Yardage is based on 45"w fabric.
- blue print — 1¼-yd
- red print — ¼-yd
- assorted fabrics for appliqués

Other supplies
- pillow form — 14" square
- paper-backed fusible web
- embroidery floss — white and black
- 2 black buttons — ³/₁₆" diameter
- 3 black buttons — ¼" diameter
- white medium rickrack — 4 12¾" lengths
- hot iron transfer pencil
- tracing paper

Refer to **Pillow Top Diagram** *as needed. See* **Quilter's Basics** *(pg. 115) for more in-depth basic instructions.*

CUTTING

Blue Print:
- For pillow front, cut 1 square 19" x 19".
- For pillow back, cut 2 rectangles 12½" x 19".
- For binding, cut 1 square 14" x 14".

Red Print:
- For trim, cut 2 strips 1¼"w.

Assorted Fabrics for Appliqués:
- Use patterns, pg. 76, and follow **Preparing Appliqué Pieces**, pg. 119, to make the following appliqués:
  - snowman head
  - snowman body
  - nose
  - cap
  - cuff
  - pom-pom
  - scarf
  - snow
  - star

PIECING

1. Follow manufacturer's instructions to fuse appliqués to background.

2. Follow **Satin Stitch Appliqué**, pg. 120, to appliqué snow, snowman body, snowman head, nose, scarf, cap, cuff, pom-pom, and star.

3. Sew trim strips together end to end. Press each long edge of trim ¼" to wrong side. Lay trim on pillow top with outside edge 2½" from edges, mitering corners and overlapping ends. Fold overlapping end to wrong side. Lay lengths of rickrack under inside edge of trim; pin in place. Topstitch trim and rickrack in place.

4. Follow manufacturer's instructions and use hot iron transfer pencil to transfer words, pg. 79, and snowflake, pg. 76, to pillow top. Refer to **Hand Stitches**, pg. 127, to Backstitch words and snowflakes. Stitch white French Knots on ends of snowflake spokes. Stitch black French Knots for snowman's mouth. Sew buttons to snowman.

5. For each pillow back piece, press 1 long edge ¼" to wrong side; press to wrong side again. Topstitch along folded edge.

6. Matching **wrong** sides and raw edges and overlapping pillow back pieces, baste pillow front to pillow back ¼" from edges. Topstitch along outside edge of trim.

7. Follow **Binding**, pg. 124, to bind pillow using a 14" square of binding fabric to make 2½-yds of 2½"w continuous bias binding with mitered corners. Insert pillow form.

Pillow Top Diagram

TULIP QUILT

(shown on pg. 24)

Finished Size: 79" x 88"
Block Size: 9" x 9"

FABRICS

Yardage is based on 45"w fabric.
• white — 4-yds
• pink — 3³/₄-yds
• green — 1¹/₂-yds
• fabric for backing and hanging sleeve — 5¹/₂-yds
• fabric for binding — 2⁵/₈-yds

Other supplies
• batting — 81" x 96"

Refer to **Quilt Top Diagram**, page 82, as needed. See **Quilter's Basics** (pg. 115) for more in-depth basic instructions.

CUTTING

White:
• Cut 9 strips 1⁵/₈"w. From this strip, cut:
  •216 small squares 1⁵/₈" x 1⁵/₈".
• Cut 15 strips 2³/₄"w. From this strip, cut:
  •216 medium squares 2³/₄" x 2³/₄".
• Use template, pg. 82, and follow **Template Cutting**, pg. 116, to cut 144 triangles; cut 144 in reverse. Mark dots.

Pink:
• Cut 9 strips 5"w. From this strip, cut:
  •72 large squares 5" x 5".
• Use template to cut 72 triangles; cut 72 in reverse. Mark dots.
• Cut 2 top/bottom borders 3¹/₂" x 76".
• Cut 2 side borders 3¹/₂" x 85".

Green:
• Cut 3 strips 1⁵/₈"w. From this strip, cut:
  •72 small squares 1⁵/₈" x 1⁵/₈".
• Use template to cut 72 triangles; cut 72 in reverse. Mark dots.

PIECING

1. Matching dots, sew 1 pink triangle and 1 white triangle together to make Unit 1. Make 72 Unit 1's. Sew 1 pink triangle and 1 white triangle together to make Unit 2. Make 72 Unit 2's.

Unit 1 – make 72   Unit 2 – make 72

2. Matching dots, sew 1 green triangle and 1 white triangle together to make Unit 3. Make 72 Unit 3's. Sew 1 green triangle and 1 white triangle together to make Unit 4. Make 72 Unit 4's.

Unit 3 – make 72   Unit 4 – make 72

3. Sew 3 small white squares and 1 small green square together to make Unit 5. Make 72 Unit 5's.

Unit 5 – make 72

4. Sew 1 medium white square, 1 Unit 1, and 1 Unit 5 together to make Unit 6. Make 72 Unit 6's.

Unit 6 – make 72

5. Sew 1 unit 3, 1 large pink square, and 1 Unit 2 together to make Unit 7. Make 72 Unit 7's.

Unit 7 – make 72

6. Sew 2 medium white squares and 1 Unit 4 together to make Unit 8. Make 72 Unit 8's.

Unit 8 – make 72

7. Sew Units 6, 7, and 8 together to make Block. Make 72 blocks.

Block – make 72

8. Sew 8 blocks together to make Row. Make 9 Rows.

Row – make 9

9. Sew 9 Rows together to make center section of Quilt Top.

10. Follow **Adding Mitered Borders**, pg. 122, to add borders to complete Quilt Top.

Quilt Top Diagram

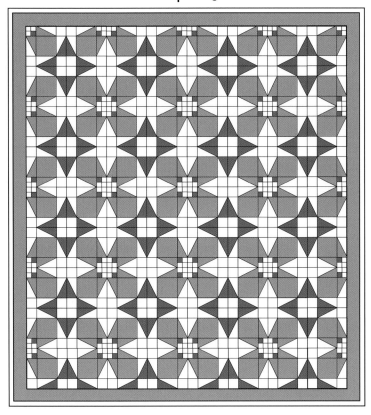

FINISHING

1. Mark, layer, and quilt as desired. Our quilt is hand quilted in intersecting diagonal lines 1" apart across the center section of the quilt top and in diagonal lines $3/8$" apart along the borders.

2. Follow **Binding,** pg. 124, to bind quilt using $9\frac{1}{2}$-yds of 1"w straight-grain binding with overlapped corners.

DOGWOOD QUILT
(shown on pg. 26)

Finished Size: 67" x 96"

FABRICS

Yardage is based on 45"w fabric.
• cream — $6\frac{1}{4}$-yds
• light pink — $1/4$-yd
• pink — $1/2$-yd
• dark pink — $1/4$-yd
• yellow — $1/4$-yd
• green — $3/8$-yd
• brown — $3/8$-yd
• fabric for backing — $6\frac{1}{4}$-yds
• fabric for binding — 3-yds
Other supplies
• batting — 81" x 96"
• embroidery floss — pink, yellow, green, and brown

*Refer to **Quilt Top Diagram** as needed. See **Quilter's Basics** (pg. 115) for more in-depth basic instructions.*

CUTTING
Cream:
• Cut two pieces of fabric 42" x 100".
Light Pink:
• Use patterns, pgs. 83 – 84, to cut the following:
  •25 petals for large flower.
  •36 petals for medium flower.
  •9 petals for small flower.

Template

Pink:
- Use patterns to cut the following:
  - 50 petals for large flower.
  - 72 petals for medium flower.
  - 18 petals for small flower.

Dark Pink:
- Use patterns to cut the following:
  - 25 petals for large flower.
  - 36 petals for medium flower.
  - 18 petals for small flower.

Yellow:
- Use pattern to cut the following:
  - 70 flower centers.

Green:
- Use patterns to cut the following:
  - 126 leaves in any combination.

Brown:
- Use patterns to cut the following:
  - 9 each of all branches.

PIECING
Note: Use 3 strands of floss for all embroidery.

1. Referring to **Choosing and Preparing the Backing**, pg. 123, use cream fabric to assemble a 3-panel quilt top with 2 vertical seams. Fold quilt top into quarters; press to mark placement guidelines and center.

2. Refer to **Quilt Top Diagram** to pin appliqués in place.

3. Using brown floss for branches, pink floss for flowers, green floss for leaves, and yellow floss for centers, refer to **Hand Stitches**, pg. 127, to Blanket Stitch appliqués to background. Use brown floss to Stem Stitch detail lines in petals, Satin Stitch tips of petals, and Straight Stitch highlights in centers. Use green floss to Stem Stitch leaf stems and detail lines in leaves.

FINISHING
1. Trim appliquéd top to 66¹/₂" x 95¹/₂". Mark, layer, and quilt as desired.

2. Follow **Binding,** pg. 124, to bind quilt using 9¹/₂ -yds of 1¹/₂"w straight-grain binding with overlapping corners.

Quilt Top Diagram

Flower Center

Small Flower

Branch

Branch

Branch

Branch

Branch

Branch

Branch

Medium Flower

Branch

Leaf

Branch

Large Flower

Leaf

Leaf

Branch

84

DOGWOOD PILLOW

(shown on pg. 27)

Finished Size: 12" x 16"

FABRICS

Yardage is based on 45"w fabric.
- cream — $1/2$-yd
- light pink — $1/8$-yd
- pink — $3/8$-yd
- dark pink — $3/8$-yd
- yellow — $1/8$-yd
- green — $1/8$-yd
- brown — $1/8$-yd

Other supplies
- batting — 45" x 60"
- $1/4$" cord
- embroidery floss — pink, yellow, green, and brown
- water-soluble fabric marking pen
- pillow form or fiberfill for stuffing

*Refer to **Pillow Top Diagram** as needed. See **Quilter's Basics** (pg. 115) for more in-depth basic instructions.*

CUTTING

Cream:
- Cut rectangle 10" x 15" for top.
- Cut rectangles $12^1/2$" x $16^1/2$" for pillow top backing and pillow backing.

Light Pink:
- Use patterns, pgs. 83 – 84, to cut:
  - 2 petals for medium flowers.
  - 1 petal for small flower.

Pink:
- Cut 2 strips $2^1/2$" x $13^1/2$.
- Cut 2 strips 2" x $12^1/2$.
- Use patterns to cut:
  - 4 petals for medium flowers.
  - 2 petals for small flower.

Dark Pink:
- Use patterns to cut:
  - 2 petals for medium flowers.
  - 1 petal for small flower.
- Cut fabric square 12" x 12" for welting.

Yellow:
- Use pattern to cut:
  - 3 centers.

Green:
- Use patterns to cut:
  - 6 leaves in any combination.

Brown:
- Use patterns to cut:
  - 3 branches.

PIECING

Note: Use 3 strands of floss for all embroidery.

1. Fold 10" x 15" rectangle into quarters; press to mark placement guidelines and center.

2. Refer to **Pillow Top Diagram** to pin appliqués in place.

3. Using brown floss for branches, pink floss for flowers, green floss for leaves, and yellow floss for centers, refer to **Hand Stitches**, pg. 127, to Blanket Stitch appliqués to background. Use brown floss to Stem Stitch detail lines in petals, Satin Stitch tips of petals, and Straight Stitch highlights in centers. Use green floss to Stem Stitch leaf stems and detail lines in leaves.

4. Trim appliquéd rectangle to $8^1/2$" x $13^1/2$".

5. Sew $2^1/2$" x $13^1/2$" strips to top and bottom of appliquéd rectangle. Sew remaining strips to sides of appliquéd rectangle.

6. Mark, layer, and quilt. Quilt in the ditch around all appliqués. Beginning with a diagonal line from corner to corner, stitch diagonal lines $7/8$" apart across background and borders.

7. Follow **Pillow Finishing**, pg. 127, to make a welted pillow.

Pillow Top Diagram

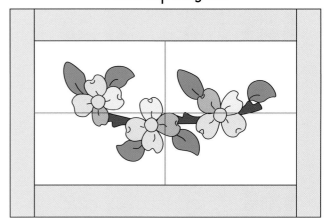

DOGWOOD WALL HANGING

(shown on pg. 27)

Finished Size: $21\frac{1}{2}$" x $21\frac{1}{2}$"

FABRICS

Yardage is based on 45"w fabric.
• cream — $\frac{5}{8}$-yd
• light pink — $\frac{1}{8}$-yd
• pink — $\frac{3}{8}$-yd
• dark pink — $\frac{1}{8}$-yd
• yellow — $\frac{1}{8}$-yd
• green — $\frac{1}{8}$-yd
• brown — $\frac{1}{8}$-yd
• fabric for binding — $\frac{1}{2}$-yd

Other supplies
• batting — 45" x 60"
• embroidery floss — pink, yellow, green, and brown
• water-soluble fabric marking pen

Refer to **Wall Hanging Diagram** *as needed. See* **Quilter's Basics** *(pg. 115) for more in-depth basic instructions.*

CUTTING
Cream:
• Cut fabric square 16" x 16" for top.
• Cut fabric square 23" x 23" for backing.
• Cut 2 strips $1\frac{1}{2}$"w. Label each as A.
• Cut 2 strips $1\frac{1}{2}$"w. Label as D and E.
• Cut fabric square $14\frac{1}{2}$" x $14\frac{1}{2}$" for binding.

Light Pink:
• Use patterns, pgs. 83 – 84, to cut:
  •2 petals for large flowers.
  •4 petals for medium flowers.

Pink:
• Cut 4 strips $1\frac{1}{2}$"w. Label two as B and two as C.
• Cut 1 strip $1\frac{1}{2}$"w. Label as F.
• Use patterns, pgs. 83 – 84, to cut:
  •4 petals for large flower.
  •8 petals for medium flower.

Dark Pink:
• Use patterns, pgs. 83 – 84, to cut:
  •2 petals for large flowers.
  •4 petals for medium flowers.

Yellow:
• Use pattern, pg. 83, to cut:
  •6 centers.

Green:
• Use patterns, pg. 84, to cut:
  •9 leaves.

Brown:
• Use patterns, pg. 84, to cut:
• 6 branches.

PIECING

Note: Use 3 strands of floss for all embroidery.

1. Fold 16" square into quarters; press to mark placement guidelines and center. Using fabric marking pen, mark an 8" diameter circle in center of square.

2. Refer to **Wall Hanging Diagram** to pin appliqués in place.

3. Using brown floss for branches, pink floss for flowers, green floss for leaves, and yellow floss for centers, refer to **Hand Stitches**, pg. 127, to Blanket Stitch appliqués to background. Use brown floss to Stem Stitch detail lines in petals, Satin Stitch tips of petals, and Straight Stitch highlights in centers. Use green floss to Stem Stitch leaf stems and detail lines in leaves.

4. Trim appliquéd square to $15\frac{1}{2}$" x $15\frac{1}{2}$".

5. Sew 1 each of strips A, B, and C together to make a Strip Set. Repeat with remaining A, B, and C. Cut across 1 strip set at $1\frac{1}{2}$" intervals to make Unit 1's. Make 4 Unit 1's. Cut across strip sets at $15\frac{1}{2}$" intervals to make Unit 2. Make 4 Unit 2's.

Strip Set

Unit 1 – make 4

Unit 2 – make 4

6. Sew strips D, E, and F together to make a Strip Set. Cut across strip set at 1½" intervals to make Unit 3's. Make 8 Unit 3's.

Strip Set

1½"

Unit 3 – make 8

7. Sew 2 Unit 3's and 1 Unit 1 together to make a 9-patch block. Make 4 9-patch blocks.

9-Patch Block

8. Sew 1 Unit 2 to each side of appliquéd square. Sew 1 9-patch block to each side of remaining Unit 2's; sew to top and bottom of appliquéd square.

FINISHING

1. Mark, layer, and quilt. Quilt in the ditch around all appliqués. Beginning with a diagonal line from corner to corner, stitch diagonal lines ⅞" apart in cream background. Quilt in the ditch along all borders.

2. Follow **Making a Hanging Sleeve**, pg. 126, to attach hanging sleeve to wall hanging.

3. Follow **Binding**, pg. 124, to bind wall hanging using a 17" square of binding fabric to make 2½-yds of 2½"w continuous bias binding with mitered corners.

Wall Hanging Diagram

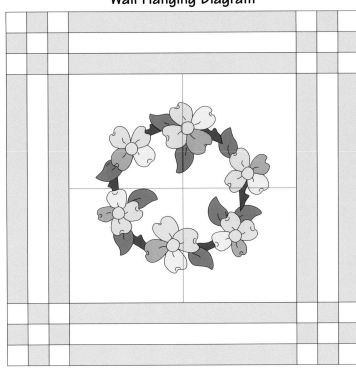

PALM LEAF PILLOW
(shown on pg. 29)

Finished Size: 14" square

FABRICS

Yardage is based on 45"w fabric.
• assorted pink, blue, yellow, green and purple prints
• white solid
• fabric for backing — ½-yd

Other supplies
• 14" pillow form

Refer to **Pillow Top Diagram,** *pg. 88, as needed. See* **Quilter's Basics** *(pg. 115) for more in-depth basic instructions.*

CUTTING

1. From each print, cut :
• 1 strip 2½"w. Randomly cut each strip in widths varying from 1½" to 4".

PIECING

1. Use patterns A and B, pg. 88, and follow **Foundation Piecing** (pg. 118) to paper piece Units A and B.

Unit A

Unit B

2. Sew Units together to complete Unit 1. Make 4 Unit 1's.

Unit 1 – make 4

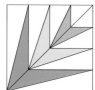

3. Sew 4 Unit 1's together to complete Block.

FINISHING

1. For pieced borders, piece strips together to form 2 short borders 2$\frac{1}{2}$" x 10$\frac{1}{2}$" and two long borders 2$\frac{1}{2}$" x 14$\frac{1}{2}$".

2. Follow **Pillow Finishing**, pg. 127, to make a knife-edge pillow.

Pillow Top Diagram

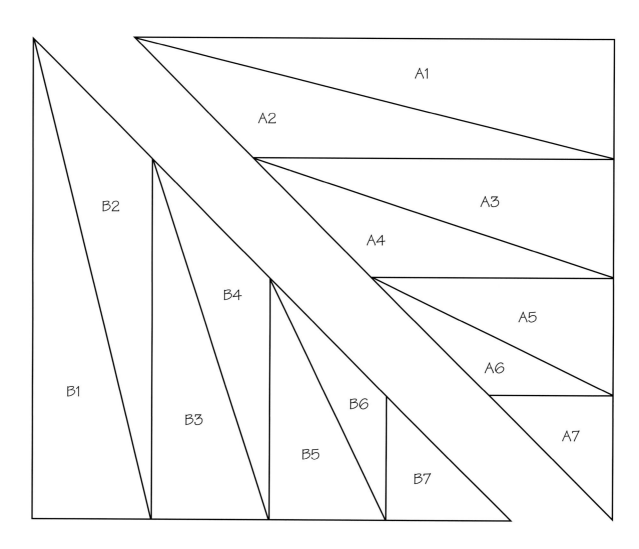

GRANDMOTHER'S FLOWER GARDEN PILLOW

(shown on pg. 29)

Finished Size: 12" square

FABRICS

Yardage is based on 45"w fabric.
- yellow, pink, and blue prints — scraps
- white solid for background, backing and ruffle — 1-yd
- fabric for welting — ½-yd

Other supplies
- freezer paper
- ¼" diameter cord
- 12" pillow form

Refer to **Pillow Top Diagram** as needed. See **Quilter's Basics** (pg. 115) for more in-depth basic instructions.

CUTTING

1. From freezer paper, use dashed line on pattern, pg. 90, to cut:
   - 19 hexagons.
2. From each print, use solid line on pattern to cut:
   - 1 yellow hexagon.
   - 6 pink hexagons.
   - 12 blue hexagons.
3. From white, cut:
   - 2 squares 12½" x 12½" for background and backing.
   - 3½"w bias strips for ruffle.

PIECING

1. Place 1 freezer paper hexagon on the wrong side of one fabric hexagon, with the waxy side of the freezer paper facing up. Use a warm, dry iron to press the seam allowances onto the paper. Repeat for remaining hexagons.

2. Matching right sides and all corners, place yellow and 1 pink hexagon together as shown in Fig. 1. Avoiding stitching through the paper, whipstitch two edges together from corner to corner along one side, backstitching at the beginning and end of the seam. Open pieces flat (Fig. 2).

Fig. 1

Fig. 2

3. Continue adding pink hexagons to the yellow hexagon, one at a time, in the same manner to make Unit 1. It is not necessary to knot and clip your thread each time you reach the end of a hexagon side.

Unit 1

4. Sew a second ring of blue hexagons around Unit 1 to make Unit 2.

Unit 2

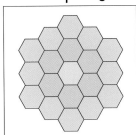

5. Remove the freezer paper from the hexagons. Following **Hand Stitches**, pg. 127, to center and Blind Stitch Unit 2 to white background to make Pillow Top.

Pillow Top Diagram

FINISHING

1. For ruffle, piece strips together to form 3½" x 120" ruffle.

2. Follow **Pillow Finishing**, pg. 127, to make a ruffled pillow with welting.

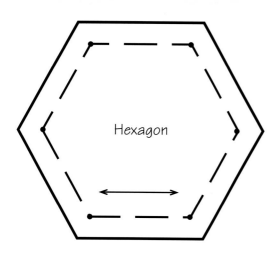

Hexagon

POT OF LILIES PILLOW

(shown on pg. 28)

Finished Size: 12" square

FABRICS

Yardage is based on 45"w fabric.
• assorted pink, blue, yellow, green and purple prints and solids
• white solid
• fabric for backing — $^3/_8$-yd
• fabric for welting — $^1/_2$-yd

Other supplies
• $^1/_4$" diameter cord
• 12" pillow form

Refer to **Pillow Top Diagram** *as needed. See* **Quilter's Basics** *(pg. 115) for more in-depth basic instructions.*

CUTTING
Purple Print:
• For Borders, cut:
 •2 strips $1^1/_2$" x $10^1/_2$" for side borders.
 •2 strips $1^1/_2$" x $12^1/_2$" for top and bottom borders.
White solid:
• For background, cut:
 •2 squares $5^7/_8$" x $5^7/_8$". Cut each square diagonally.

PIECING
1. Use patterns A-F, pgs. 91 – 92, and follow **Foundation Piecing** (pg. 118) to paper piece Units A-F.

2. Sew Units together to complete Unit 1.

Unit 1

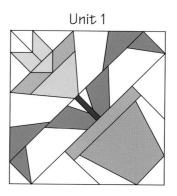

3. Sew 1 white triangle to each side of Unit 1 to complete Unit 2.

Unit 2

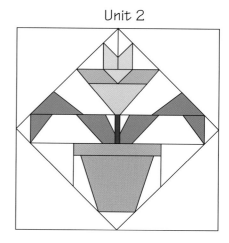

FINISHING
1. Sew side then top and bottom borders to Unit 2 to complete Pillow Top.

Pillow Top Diagram

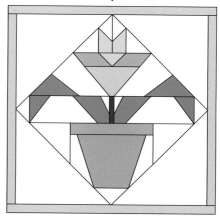

2. Follow **Pillow Finishing**, pg. 127, to make welted pillow.

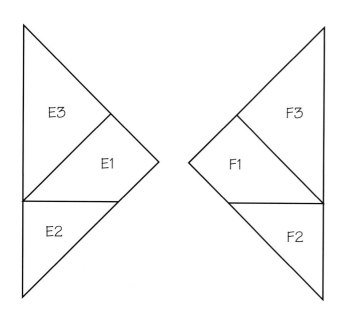

ARTWORK WALL HANGING
(shown on pg. 30)

FABRICS

- white solid
- assorted fabrics for frames
- assorted fabrics for backgrounds
- fabric for inner border
- fabric for outer border
- fabric for backing
- fabric for binding

Other supplies

- batting – 45" x 60"
- child's artwork and/or photographs
- photograph transfer paper — for color copiers **or** for inkjet printers
- desired embellishments

Refer to **Wall Hanging Top Diagram** *as needed. See* **Quilter's Basics** *(pg. 115) for more in-depth basic instructions.*

PIECING

Use 1/4" seam allowances throughout.

1. Follow manufacturer's instructions to transfer artwork and/or photos to white fabric; trim to desired sizes, allowing 1/4" seam allowance on each side.

2. To frame each piece of artwork, cut side frame strips the same length as sides of artwork and the desired width. (Our frame strips were cut 1³/₄"w for

a 1¹/₄" finished frame.) Sew frame strips to sides. Cut top and bottom frame strips the length of top and the desired width. Sew frame strips to top and bottom.

3. Working on a flat surface, arrange framed artwork in rows as desired. (**Hint:** The artwork will be easier to work with if the framed artwork in each row is the same height.) Some fabric backgrounds may need to be cut to complete rows. Determine size needed and add seam allowances.

4. Sew framed artwork and backgrounds together to complete rows. Sew rows together to complete center of wall hanging.

5. Embellish as desired. We added our budding artist's photo by sewing frame strips to each side of the photo, pressing under raw edges, and topstitching it in place. We sewed buttons to each corner. She signed her work and drew a perky little flower on one of our fabric backgrounds and we Backstitched over her signature using 3 strands of embroidery floss. Our little artist had experimented with crayon shavings melted between two layers of waxed paper and framed with a construction paper heart. We copied the heart, cut it out, Blanket Stitched it to the wall hanging, and added a ribbon bow and button for just the right finishing touch.

6. Cut inner top and bottom borders as long as the center of the wall hanging and the desired width. (Our borders were cut 1¹/₄"w for a ³/₄" finished border.) Sew borders to top and bottom. Cut inner side borders as long as the center of the wall hanging with borders added and the desired width. Sew borders to sides.

7. Cut outer top and bottom borders as long as the center of the wall hanging with inner borders added and the desired width. (Our borders were cut 2³/₄"w for a 2¹/₄" finished border.) Sew borders to top and bottom. Cut outer side borders as long as the center of the wall hanging with borders added and the desired width. Sew borders to sides.

FINISHING

1. Mark, layer, and quilt wall hanging. We quilted in the ditch around all artwork, frames, and borders.

2. Follow **Making a Hanging Sleeve**, pg. 126, to attach hanging sleeve to wall hanging.

3. Follow **Binding**, pg. 124, to bind wall hanging using 2¹/₂"w continuous bias binding with mitered corners.

Wall Hanging Top Diagram

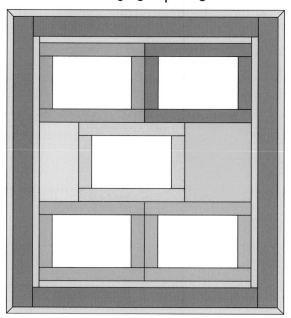

ANNIVERSARY WALL HANGING
(shown on pg. 31)

Finished Size: 39¹/₂" x 39¹/₂"

FABRICS

Yardage is based on 45"w fabric.
• white solid — ¹/₂-yd
• yellow solid — ¹/₄-yd
• small yellow print for outer borders — 1-yd
• yellow floral print — ¹/₂-yd
• light blue print for vines — ⁵/₈-yd
• medium blue print — ⁵/₈-yd
• dark blue print for inner borders — ³/₄-yd
• fabric for backing — 1¹/₄-yds
• fabric for binding — ⁵/₈-yd

Other supplies
• batting – 45" x 60"
• photographs
• photo transfer paper — for color copiers **or** for inkjet printers
• embroidery floss — blue
• black permanent fabric marker
• template plastic

*Refer to **Wall Hanging Top Diagram**, pg. 94, as needed. See **Quilter's Basics** (pg. 115) for more in-depth basic instructions.*

CUTTING

White Solid:
• Cut 10 squares 4¹/₂" x 4¹/₂".
• Cut 4 squares 6" x 6".

Yellow Solid:
• Cut 4 strips 1³/₄"w.
• Cut 2 squares 4" x 4".

Small Yellow Print:
• Cut 2 rectangles 8" x 24".
• Cut 2 rectangles 8" x 39".

Yellow Floral Print:
• Cut 4 strips 1³/₄"w.
• Use patterns, page 95, and follow **Preparing Appliqué Pieces**, page 119, to make the following appliqués.
  • 8 small leaves
  • 4 large leaves

Light Blue Print:
• Refer to **Making Continuous Bias Strip Binding**, pg. 124, to cut 1¹/₂" w strips 4¹/₂ yds long.

Medium Blue Print:
• Cut 4 strips 1³/₄"w.
• Use patterns to make the following appliqués.
  • 12 small flowers
  • 4 large flowers

Dark Blue Print:
• Cut 2 strips 1" x 23".
• Cut 2 strips 1" x 24".

PIECING

1. Follow manufacturer's instructions to transfer photographs to white fabric squares.

2. Sew 2 medium blue print strips and 1 yellow solid strip together to make Strip Set A. Make 2 Strip Set A's. Cut across Strip Sets at 4¹/₄" intervals to make Unit 1's. Make 18 Unit 1's.

Strip Set A

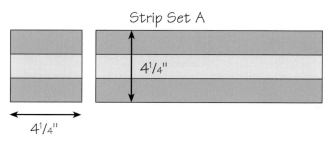

4¹/₄"

4¹/₄"

Unit 1 – make 18

93

3. Sew 2 yellow floral print strips and 1 yellow solid strip together to make Strip Set B. Make 2 Strip Set B's. Cut across Strip Sets at 4¹/₄" intervals to make Unit 2. Make 18 Unit 2's.

Strip Set B

Unit 2 – make 18

4. Sew 3 Unit 1's and 3 Unit 2's together to make a Row. Make 6 rows.

Row – make 6

5. Sew Rows together to make Unit 3.

Unit 3

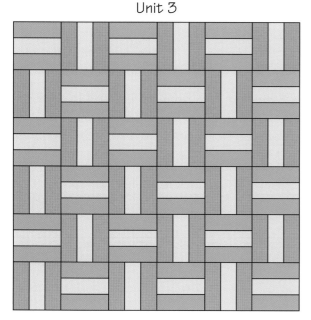

6. Sew dark blue print strips to each side of Unit 3. Sew remaining inner border strips to top and bottom.

7. Sew small yellow print rectangles to each side of Unit 3. Sew remaining outer border strips to top and bottom.

8. Cut 2 4" diameter circles from solid yellow fabric squares. Refer to **Hand Stitches**, pg. 127, to Chain Stitch year using 3 strands of floss. Scatter French Knots around numbers using 3 strands of floss.

9. Fold bias strip for vine in half lengthwise; stitch ¹/₄" from long raw edges. Press strip with seam allowance centered on 1 side. Cut vine into 4 equal pieces.

10. Cut 3³/₄" circles for small flowers and 5³/₈" circles for large flowers from transferred photos.

11. Follow **Needle-Turn Appliqué**, pg. 120, to appliqué photos to centers of flowers; appliqué vine, leaves, and flowers to border.

FINISHING

1. Mark, layer, and quilt wall hanging. Quilt-in-the-ditch around all rectangles in center, along each side of inner border, and around all flowers, leaves, and vines.

2. Follow **Making a Hanging Sleeve**, pg. 126, to attach hanging sleeve to wall hanging.

3. Follow **Binding,** pg. 124, to bind wall hanging using a 22" square of binding fabric to make 4¹/₂-yds of 2¹/₂"w continuous bias binding with mitered corners.

4. Have friends use black permanent pen to write their sentiments on the solid yellow rectangles of the quilt.

Wall Hanging Top Diagram

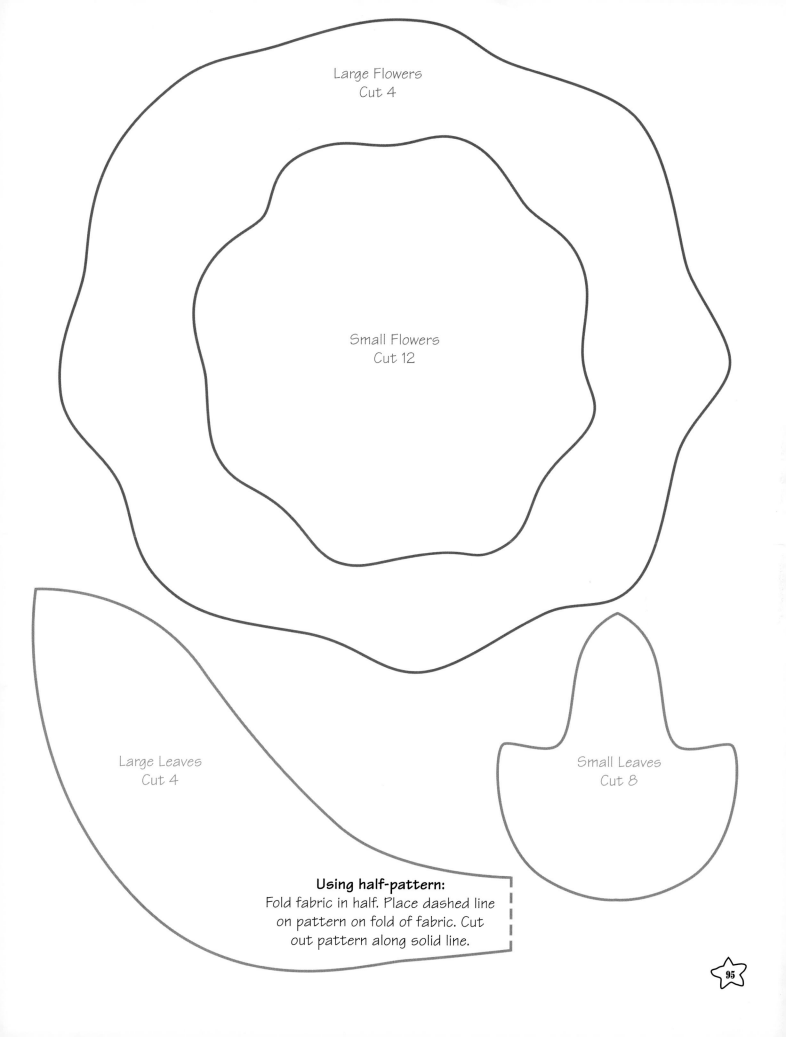

Large Flowers
Cut 4

Small Flowers
Cut 12

Large Leaves
Cut 4

Small Leaves
Cut 8

Using half-pattern:
Fold fabric in half. Place dashed line on pattern on fold of fabric. Cut out pattern along solid line.

TRIP AROUND THE WORLD QUILT

(shown on pg. 32)

Finished Size: 77³/₄" x 77³/₄"

FABRICS

Yardage is based on 45"w fabric.

- green fabric for outer borders — 2¹/₂-yds
- yellow fabric for middle borders — 2³/₈-yds
- red fabric for inner borders — 2¹/₄-yds
- dark blue, medium blue, light blue, red, dark pink, medium pink, light pink, olive green, dark green, medium green, light green, and orange — ¹/₂-yd each
- dark yellow, medium yellow, light yellow, and navy — ³/₄-yd each
- fabric for backing and hanging sleeve — 5-yds
- fabric for binding — ⁷/₈-yd

Other supplies

- batting — 90" x 108"

Refer to **Assembly Diagram**, *pg. 98, as needed. See* **Quilter's Basics** *(pg. 115) for more in-depth basic instructions.*

CUTTING

Green:

- Cut 2 side outer borders 3" x 77¹/₄".
- Cut 2 lengthwise top/bottom outer borders 3" x 82¹/₄".

Yellow:

- Cut 2 lengthwise side middle borders 2¹/₂" x 73¹/₄".
- Cut 2 lengthwise top/bottom middle borders 2¹/₂" x 77¹/₄".
- Cut 8 2¹/₄"w strips.

Red:

- Cut 2 lengthwise side inner borders 2¹/₂" x 69¹/₄".
- Cut 2 lengthwise top/bottom inner borders 2¹/₂" x 73¹/₄".

Orange:

- Cut 1 square 2¹/₄" x 2¹/₄" for center square.

Dark blue, medium blue, light blue, red, dark pink, medium pink, light pink, olive green, dark green, medium green, light green, and orange:

- Cut 5 2¹/₄"w strips from *each* fabric.

Dark yellow, medium yellow, and navy:

- Cut 6 2¹/₄"w strips from *each* fabric.

Light Yellow

- Cut 8 2¹/₄"w strips.

PIECING

1. Sew strips together in color order shown to make Strip Set 1. Make 5 Strip Sets.

Strip Set 1 - make 5

| medium yellow |
| light yellow |
| navy |
| dark blue |
| medium blue |
| light blue |
| red |
| dark pink |
| medium pink |
| light pink |
| dark green |
| medium green |
| light green |
| orange |
| dark yellow |

2. With right sides together and matching long raw edges, sew final lengthwise seam of Strip Set to form a tube (Fig. 1). Repeat with remaining Strip Sets.

Fig. 1

3. Referring to Fig. 2, cut across Strip Sets at 2¹/₄" intervals to make 84 circular Strip Units.

Fig. 2

Strip Unit - make 84

4. Refer to Section diagrams to determine which color square to place at the top of each Strip Unit. Use a seam ripper to remove seam above determined top square of each Strip Unit (Fig. 3). Working from left to right on a flat surface, carefully arrange Strip Units in correct order to make each Section A. Make 4 Section A's.

Fig. 3

Section A - make 4

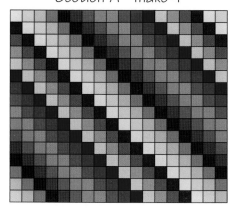

5. Carefully arrange Strip Units in correct order to make each Section B. Make 4 Section B's.

Section B - make 4

6. Sew 1 medium yellow, 2 light yellow, and 1 navy square together to make each Section C. Make 4 Section C's.

Section C - make 4

7. Use a seam ripper to remove seam above determined top of square of one strip set unit to make Section D. Make 4 Section D's.

Section D - make 4

8. Sew 1 Section C to each Section B. Sew Section A's, Section B/C's, Section D's and Center Square together to make center section of quilt top.

9. Follow **Adding Squared Borders**, page 121, to add side, then top and bottom inner borders to center section. Repeat to add middle and outer borders to complete Quilt Top.

FINISHING

1. Mark, layer, and quilt as desired. Our quilt is hand quilted in diagonal lines across the pieced-square section and in the ditch along each border.

2. Follow **Binding,** pg. 124, to bind quilt using a 30" square of binding fabric to make $8^{3}/_{4}$-yds of $2^{1}/_{2}$"w continuous bias binding with overlapping corners.

Assembly Diagram

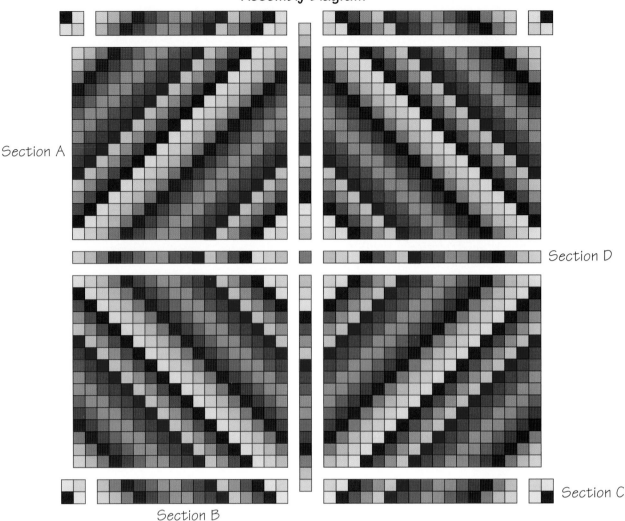

Section A

Section D

Section B

Section C

ACORN LAP THROW

(shown on pg. 33)

Finished Size: 47³/₄" x 47³/₄"
Block Size: 15" x 15"

FABRICS

Yardage is based on 45"w fabric.
• light gold print — 1¹/₂-yds
• 8 different medium gold prints — 10" x 18" each
• green stripe — ³/₈-yd
• medium green print — ³/₈-yd
• dark green print — ³/₄-yd
• red print — ³/₈-yd
• 4 different black prints — 16" x 16" each
• fabric for backing and hanging sleeve — 3-yds
• fabric for binding — 1¹/₂-yds

Other supplies
• batting — 45" x 60"

Refer to **Quilt Top Diagram,** *as needed. See* **Quilter's Basics** *(pg. 115) for more in-depth basic instructions.*

CUTTING
Light Gold Print:
• Cut 4 lengthwise strips 8"w. From these strips, cut:
  • 2 borders 8" x 32³/₄".
  • 2 borders 8" x 47³/₄".

Variety of medium gold prints:
• From each print, cut 2 squares 8" x 8".

Green Stripe:
• Cut 6 strips 1¹/₄"w. From these strips, cut:
  • 2 strips 1¹/₄" x 15¹/₂".
  • 3 strips 1¹/₄" x 31¹/₄".
  • 2 strips 1¹/₄" x 32³/₄".

Medium Green Print:
• Use patterns, pg. 100, to cut:
  • 20 acorn caps.
  • 4 bud caps.

Dark Green Print:
• Follow **Making Continuous Bias Strip Binding**, pg. 124, to cut:
  • 1 square 18" x 18". From this square cut:
  • 1 bias strip 1½" x 180".
• Use pattern to cut:
  • 16 stems.

Red Print:
• Use patterns to cut:
  • 20 acorns.
  • 4 buds.

Variety of Black Prints:
• Use pattern to cut:
  • 4 oak leaves.

PIECING

1. Sew 4 gold print squares together to make Unit 1. Make 4 Unit 1's.

Unit 1 – make 4

2. Follow **Needle-Turn Appliqué**, pg. 120, to appliqué stems, acorn caps, acorns, and oak leaves to Unit 1's.

3. (Note: Appliqués are not shown in Steps 3-6.) Sew 2 Unit 1's and a 1¼" x 15½" strip together to make Unit 2. Make 2 Unit 2's.

Unit 2 – make 2

4. Sew 2 Unit 2's and a 1¼" x 31¼" strip together to make Unit 3.

Unit 3

5. Sew 1¼" x 31¼" strips to sides. Sew remaining strips to top and bottom of Unit 3 to make Unit 4.

Unit 4

6. Sew borders to sides, then top and bottom of Unit 4 to make Unit 5.

Unit 5

7. Matching wrong sides, fold dark green bias strip in half. Use a ¼" seam allowance to sew along long edge. Centering seam, press strip. Pin bias strip and appliqués in place. Topstitch bias strip to throw along edges. Appliqué acorn, acorn caps, buds, and bud caps to border to make Quilt Top.

FINISHING

1. Mark, layer, and quilt wall hanging.

2. Follow **Making a Hanging Sleeve**, pg. 126, to attach hanging sleeve to wall hanging.

3. Follow **Binding**, pg. 124, to bind wall hanging using 6-yds of 2½"w straight-grain binding with mitered corners.

Quilt Top Diagram

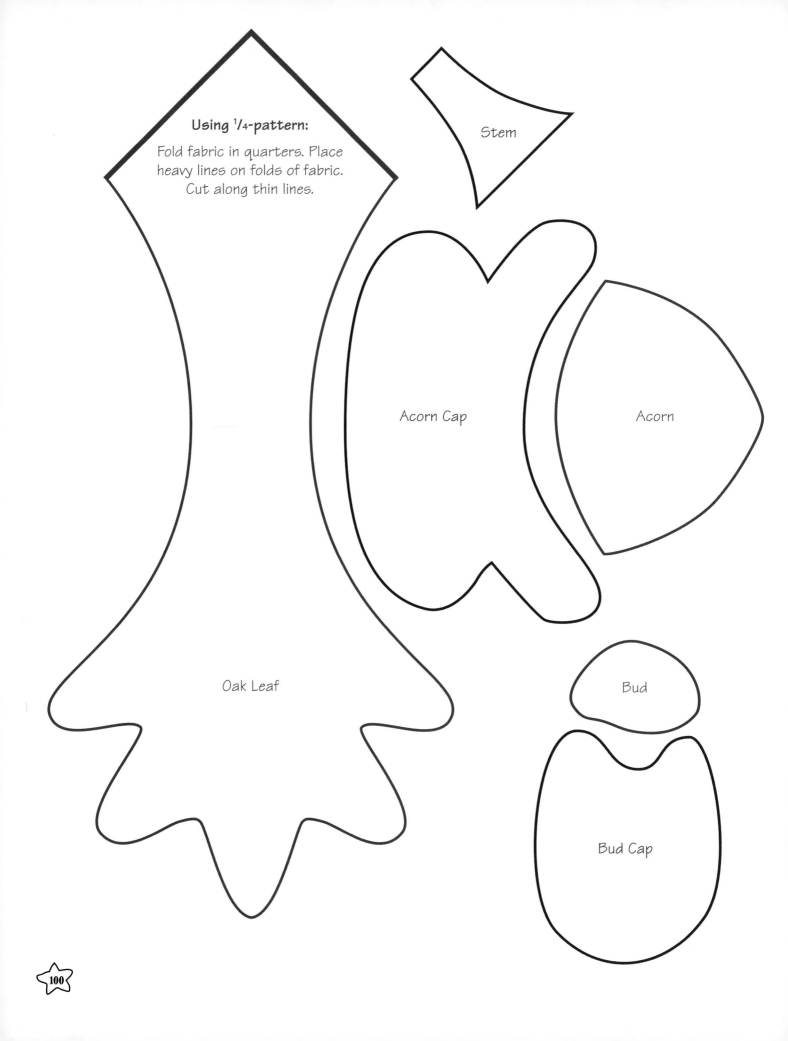

Using ¹/₄-pattern:

Fold fabric in quarters. Place heavy lines on folds of fabric. Cut along thin lines.

Stem

Acorn Cap

Acorn

Oak Leaf

Bud

Bud Cap

ACORN WREATH

(shown on pg. 34)

Wreath Size: 18" diameter
Acorn Size: 4½" x 5"

FABRICS

Yardage is based on 45"w fabric.
• 3 different green print fabrics — ¼-yd each
• red print — ¼-yd

Supplies

• batting — ¼-yd
• grapevine wreath — 18" diameter
• assorted artificial leaves and flowers
• hot glue gun and glue sticks

CUTTING

Green Prints:

• For backing, cut 7 squares 6" x 6".
• Use pattern to cut:
  •7 acorn caps.

Red Print:

• Use pattern to cut:
  •7 acorns.

Batting:

• Cut 7 squares 6" x 6"

PIECING

1. For each acorn, place cap on top of acorn, overlapping edges ¼". Zigzag stitch along the edge to hold the two pieces together.

2. Place batting square on work surface. Place backing square right side up on top of batting. Lay acorn face down on top of batting and backing. Sew around edge of acorn, leaving an opening for turning. Trim backing and batting even with edges of acorn. Clip curves.

3. Turn acorn right side out; press. Sew opening closed.

4. Follow **Mock Hand Appliqué**, pg. 121, Steps. 2 – 6, to stitch around outside edge of acorn.

5. Glue artificial leaves, flowers, and fabric acorns to wreath as desired.

Acorn Cap
Cut 7

Acorn
Cut 7

ACORN MANTEL SCARF

(shown on pg. 34)

Finished Size: 54"w with 13½" drop
Block Size: 9½" x 9½"

FABRICS

Yardage is based on 45"w fabric.
- gold print #1 — ³/₈-yd
- gold print #2 — 1³/₄-yds
- gold print #3 — ³/₈-yd
- green print — ¼-yd
- red print — ¼-yd
- assorted black prints — ½-yd total

Refer to **Mantel Scarf Top Diagram** *as needed. See* **Quilter's Basics** *(pg. 115) for more in-depth basic instructions.*

CUTTING

Gold Print #1:
- Cut 1 square 10" x 10".

Gold Print #2:
- Cut 1 rectangle 23" x 56".
- Cut 1 rectangle 7" x 54½".
- Cut 2 squares 10⁷/₈" x 10⁷/₈". Cut these squares in half diagonally. Discard 1 half.
- Cut 1 square 10"x 10".

Gold Print #3:
- Cut 1 square 10⁷/₈" x 10⁷/₈". Cut these squares in half diagonally.
- Cut 2 squares 10"x 10".

Green Print:
- Use patterns, pg. 103 to cut:
  - 16 acorn caps.
  - 16 stems.

Red Print:
- Use pattern to cut:
  - 16 acorns.

Black Print:
- Use pattern to cut:
  - 4 oak leaves.

PIECING

1. Follow **Mock Hand Appliqué**, pg. 121, to appliqué stems, acorn caps, acorns, and oak leaves to 10" squares.

2. With appliquéd block turned on point, sew 1 triangle to top left side of each block to make Unit 1. Make 4 Unit 1's.

Unit 1 – make 4

3. Sew 1 triangle to top right side of 1 Unit 1 to make Unit 2.

Unit 2

4. Sew 3 Unit 1's and Unit 2 together to make Unit 3.

Unit 3

5. Trim top edge so it is straight. Trim side triangles at a right angle to the top edge.

6. Sew the 7" x 54½" strip to the top of Unit 3 to make Mantel Scarf Top.

Mantel Scarf Top Diagram

FINISHING

1. Matching right sides and long edges, stitching ¼" from edges of mantel scarf top, and leaving an opening for turning, sew mantel scarf top to remaining rectangle.

2. Trimming even with edges of mantel scarf top, trim excess fabric.

3. Turn mantel scarf right side out; press. Sew opening closed.

4. Topstitch ¼" from edges of mantel scarf.

5. Mark and quilt the block and triangle portion of the mantel scarf as desired.

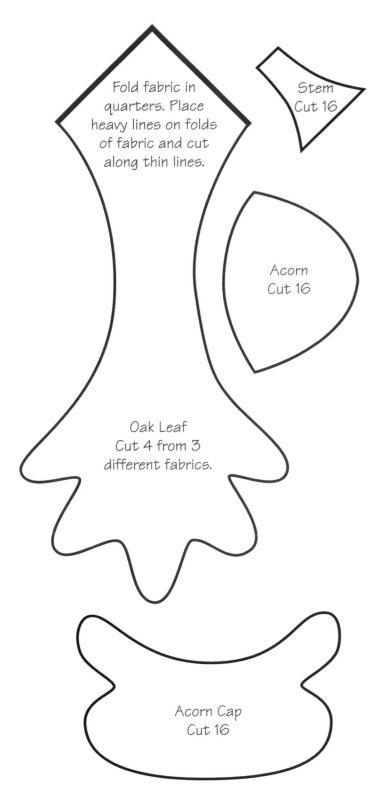

Fold fabric in quarters. Place heavy lines on folds of fabric and cut along thin lines.

Stem
Cut 16

Acorn
Cut 16

Oak Leaf
Cut 4 from 3
different fabrics.

Acorn Cap
Cut 16

ACORN BLOCK PILLOW

(shown on pg. 35)

Finished Size: 15½" square

FABRICS

Yardage is based on 45"w fabric.
• gold print #1 — ⅜-yd
• gold print #2 — ⅜-yd
• green print — ¼-yd

• red print — ¼-yd
• black print — ½-yd
• fabric for backing — ½-yd

Supplies
• batting
• 16" pillow form

*Refer to **Pillow Top Diagram** as needed. See **Quilter's Basics** (pg. 115) for more in-depth basic instructions.*

CUTTING

Gold Print #1:
• Cut 2 squares 8" x 8".

Gold Print #2:
• Cut 2 squares 8" x 8".

Green Print:
• Use patterns, pg. 100 to cut:
  • 4 acorn caps.
  • 4 stems.

Red Print:
• Use pattern, pg. 100 to cut:
  • 4 acorns.

Black Print:
• Use pattern, pg. 100 to cut:
  • 1 oak leaves.

Fabric for backing:
• Cut 2 rectangles 11" x 15½".

PIECING

1. Follow **Acorn Lap Throw**, pg. 98, Step 1 to make pillow top. Follow **Mock Hand Appliqué**, pg. 121, to appliqué stems, acorn caps, acorns, and oak leaf to pillow top.

2. Mark, layer, and stipple-quilt pillow top.

3. Press 1 long side of each backing piece ¼" to wrong side; press to wrong side again. Stitch along fold.

4. Matching right sides and raw edges and overlapping backing pieces, sew backing to pillow top. Turn right side out. Insert pillow form.

Pillow Top Diagram

103

TRIP AROUND THE WORLD PILLOW

(shown on pg. 35)

Finished Size: 12" x 20½"

FABRICS

Yardage is based on 45"w fabric.
• gold print #1 — scrap
• gold print #2 — scrap
• gold print #3 — scrap
• gold print #4 — scrap
• green print #1 — scrap
• green print #2 — scrap
• red print #1 — scrap
• red print #2 — scrap
• fabric for buttons — scraps
• fabric for backing — ½-yd
Supplies
• 12" x 16" pillow form
• 6 buttons to cover — ¾" diameter

Refer to **Pillow Top Diagram** *as needed. See* **Quilter's Basics** *(pg. 115) for more in-depth basic instructions.*

CUTTING
Gold Print #1:
• Cut 1 square 2¼" x 2¼".
Gold Print #2:
• Cut 4 squares 2¼" x 2¼".
Gold Print #3:
• Cut 2 strips 2⅛" x 12¾".
• Cut 2 strips 2¼" x 12½".
Gold Print #4:
• Cut 2 rectangles 5½" 24½".
Green Print #1:
• Cut 8 squares 2¼" x 2¼".
Green Print #2:
• Cut 10 squares 2¼" x 2¼".
Red Print #1:
• Cut 8 squares 2¼" x 2¼".
Red Print #2:
• Cut 4 squares 2¼" x 2¼".
Fabric for backing:
• Cut 1 rectangle 16¼" x 12½".

PIECING
1. Sew 2 red #2 squares, 2 red #1 squares, 2 green #2 squares and 1 green #1 square together to make Unit 1. Make 2 Unit 1's.

2. Sew 2 red #1 squares, 2 green #2 squares, 2 green #1 squares, and 1 gold #2 square together to make Unit 2. Make 2 Unit 2's.

Unit 2 — make 2

3. Sew 2 green #2 squares, 2 green #1 squares, 2 gold #2 squares, and 1 gold #1 square together to make Unit 3.

Unit 3

4. Sew Units together to make Unit 4.

Unit 4

5. Sew narrow gold #3 strips to long sides of Unit 4. Sew remaining gold #3 strips to short ends of Unit 4.

6. Matching right sides and raw edges, sew Unit 4 to backing along long edges to make pillow top.

7. Matching right sides and raw edges, sew short ends of 1 gold #4 strip together to form loop. Press strip in half lengthwise; baste raw edges together. Matching right side of loop to right side of pillow top, sew loop to pillow top. Repeat with remaining gold #4 strip.

8. Insert pillow form. Follow manufacturer's instructions to cover buttons. Sew buttons to ends of pillow through all layers.

Pillow Top Diagram

AROUND THE WORLD TABLE MAT

(shown on pg. 36)

Finished Size: 19¼" x 33¼"

FABRICS

Yardage is based on 45"w fabric.
- orange, yellow #1, yellow #2, yellow #3, green #1, green #2, green #3, green #4, red #1, red #2, red #3, gold #1, gold #2, gold #3 — ¼-yd **each**
- fabric for backing — ⅝-yd
- fabric for binding — ½-yd

Supplies
- batting — 45" x 60"

Refer to **Assembly Diagram**, *pg. 106, as needed. See* **Quilter's Basics** *(pg. 115) for more in-depth basic instructions.*

CUTTING

orange:
- Cut one 2¼" square for center.
- Cut one 2¼" strip.

yellow #1:
- Cut one 2¼" x 12" strip.

yellow #2 and #3:
- Cut 2 strips 2¼"w from **each** fabric. From strips, cut:
  - 2 strips 2¼" x 12" and 2 strips 2¼" x 21".

green #1, green #2, green #3, green #4, red #1, and red #2:
- Cut 2 strips 2¼"w from **each** fabric. From strips, cut:
  - 2¼" x 12" strip.
  - 2¼" x 21" strip.
  - 2¼" x 30" strip.

red #3 and gold #1:
- Cut 1 strip 2¼"w from **each** fabric. From strip, cut:
  - 2¼" x 21" strip.
  - 2¼" x 30" strip.

gold #2 and #3:
- Cut one 2¼" strip from **each** fabric.

PIECING

1. Sew 12" strips together in color order shown to make Strip Set 1. Make 1 Strip Set. Cut across Strip Sets at 2¼" intervals to make 4 Strip Units. Leave 2 Strip Units in tact to make 2 Unit 1's. From remaining Strip Units, remove seam above green #3. Discard green #3, green #4, red #1, and red #2 to make Unit 2's. Make 2 Unit 2's.

	yellow #1
	yellow #2
	yellow #3
	green #1
16¼"	green #2
	green #3
	green #4
	red #1
	red #2

2¼"

Unit 1 – make 2

Unit 2 – make 2

2. Sew 21" strips together in color order shown to make Strip Set 2. Make 1 Strip Set. Cut across Strip Sets at 2¼" intervals to make 8 Strip Units. From four Strip Units, remove seam above gold #1. Discard gold #1 to make Unit 3. Make 4 Unit 3's. From remaining Strip Units, remove seam above yellow #3. Discard yellow #2 to make Unit 4. Make 4 Unit 4's.

Strip Set 2 - make 1

	yellow #2
	yellow #3
	green #1
18"	green #2
	green #3
	green #4
	red #1
	red #2
	red #3
	gold #1

2¼"

Unit 3 – make 4

Unit 4 – make 4

3. Sew 30" strips together in color order shown to make Strip Set 3. Make 1 Strip Set. Cut across Strip Sets at 2¼" intervals to make 12 Strip Units. From four Strip Units, remove seam above gold #3. Discard gold #3 and orange to make Unit 5. Make 4 Unit 5's. From four Strip Units, remove seam above green #2 and orange. Discard green #1 and orange to make Unit 6. Make 4 Unit 6's. From remaining Strip Units, remove seam above green #3. Discard green #1 and #2 to make Unit 7. Make 4 Unit 7's.

Strip Set 3 - make 1

green #1
green #2
green #3
green #4
red #1
19³/₄" red #2
red #3
gold #1
gold #2
gold #3
orange

2¼"

Unit 5 – make 4

Unit 6 – make 4

Unit 7 – make 4

4. Refer to Quarter Section diagrams to determine placement of each Unit. Working from left to right on a flat surface, carefully arrange Units in correct order. Sew Units together to make 2 Quarter Section A's and 2 Quarter Section B's.

Quarter Section A – make 2

Quarter Section B – make 2

5. Referring to **Assembly Diagram,** sew Quarter Section A's, Quarter Section B's, Units, and Center Square together to make center section of quilt top.

Assembly Diagram

FINISHING

1. Mark, layer, and quilt as desired. Our table mat is hand quilted in diagonal lines across the pieced-square section.

2. Follow **Binding**, pg. 124, to bind quilt using an 18" square of binding fabric to make 3-yds of 2½"w continuous bias binding with overlapping corners.

CRAFT KEEPER
(shown on pg. 37)

FABRICS

Yardage is based on 45"w fabric.
• gold print — ³/₈-yd
• green print — ¼-yd
• red print — ¼-yd
• black print— ³/₈-yd

Supplies
• paper-backed fusible web
• folding craft tote

CUTTING

Use Acorn Lap Throw patterns, page 100, and follow **Preparing Appliqué Pieces**, page 119, to make the following appliqués:

Gold Print:
• Cut 1 square 10¼" x 10¼"

Green Print:
• 4 acorn caps
• 4 stems

Red Print:
• 4 acorns

Black Print:
• 1 oak leaf

INSTRUCTIONS

1. Follow manufacturer's instructions to fuse appliqués to side of craft tote.

BUTTON WALL HANGING
(shown on pg. 38)

Finished Size: 9½" x 12½"

FABRICS

Yardage is based on 45"w fabric.
• cream solid for background — ¼-yd
• 4 assorted plaids for borders — ⅛-yd of each
• fabric for backing and hanging sleeve — ³/₈-yd

Other Supplies
• batting — 13" x 16"
• 5" dia. doily
• embroidery floss — brown, yellow, gold
• hot-iron transfer pen
• tracing paper
• fabric marking pen
• rick rack
• assorted buttons

CUTTING

All measurements include a ¼" seam allowance.

Cream Solid:
• Cut 1 rectangle 8" x 10" for background.

Assorted Plaids:
• Cut 2 short side borders 2½" x 8½".
• Cut 1 top border 2½" x 10½".
• Cut 1 bottom border 3½" x 10½".

Backing and Hanging Sleeve Fabric:
• Cut 1 piece 10" x 4½" for hanging sleeve.
• Cut 1 piece 10½" X 13½" for backing.

PIECING

1. Trace basket pattern, pg. 108, onto tracing paper. Follow manufacturer's instructions and use hot-iron transfer pencil to transfer pattern to background fabric.

2. Refer to **Hand Stitches**, pg. 127, to Stem Stitch basket. For flowers within handle, use marking pen to draw around various buttons. Remove button and Blanket Stitch along drawn line, varying the length of the stitches. Sew buttons to basket and within handle.

3. Cutting lower edge ¼" below base of basket, trim background to 6½" x 8½".

4. To complete wall hanging top, sew side borders to background. Sew top border to background. Cut doily in half. Matching raw edges and centering doily along 1 long edge of border, baste doily to border. Sew bottom border to background. Whipstitch loose edge of doily in place.

5. Follow **Making A Hanging Sleeve**, pg. 126, to sew hanging sleeve to one short edge of backing piece.

6. Cut 2 10½" lengths and 2 13½" lengths of rick rack. Centering rick rack along ¼" seamline, baste 1 length to each edge of wall hanging top.

7. Matching right sides and raw edges, place backing and top on a flat work surface; lay batting on top. Sew around 4 sides, leaving an opening for turning; turn. Sew opening closed.

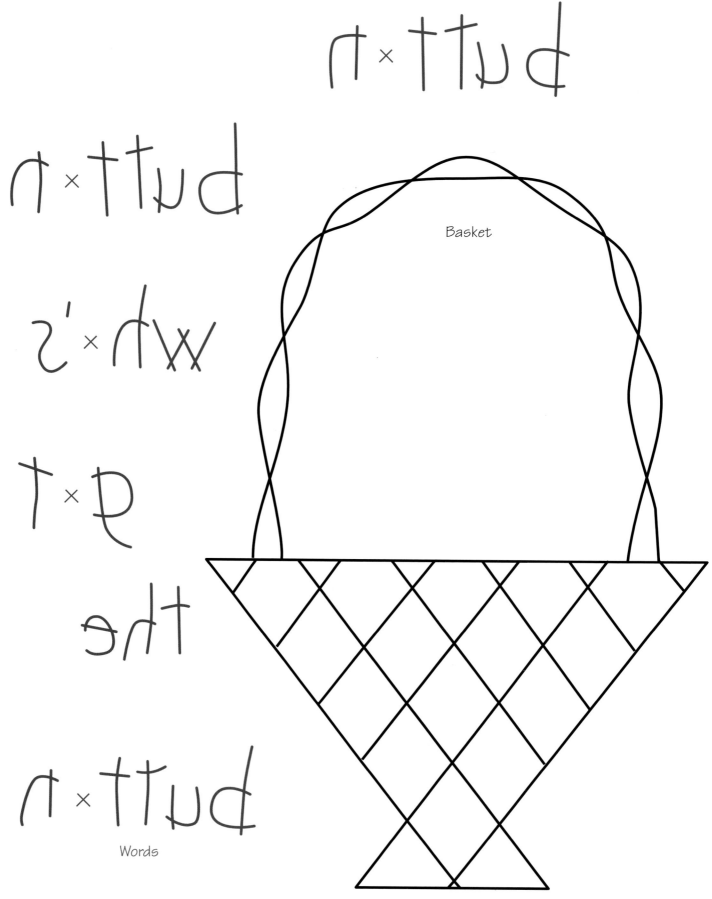

Basket

button

button

wh's?

qt

the

button

Words

BUTTON PILLOW

(shown on pg. 39)

Finished Size: 12" square

FABRICS

Yardage is based on 45"w fabric.
- cream solid — 1/8-yd
- assorted plaids — scraps of each
- fabric for backing — 3/8-yd

Other Supplies
- 12" pillow form **or** polyester fiberfill
- 2 5" dia. cotton doilies
- embroidery floss — brown
- hot-iron transfer pen
- tracing paper
- black rick rack — 1 1/2-yds
- assorted buttons
- tea bag

CUTTING

All measurements include a 1/4" seam allowance.

Cream Solid:
- Cut 6 rectangles 4" x 6".
- Cut 4 corner squares 2 3/4" x 2 3/4".

Assorted Plaids:
- Cut 4 borders 2 3/4" x 8".
- Cut 12 strips 1 3/4"w and various lengths.

Backing Fabric:
- Cut 1 square 12 1/2" x 12 1/2".

PIECING

1. Steep 1 tea bag in 2 cups of hot water; allow to cool. Immerse cream fabric and doilies into tea. Soak until desired color is achieved. Remove from tea and allow to dry. Press if desired.

2. Trace each word pattern, pg. 108, onto tracing paper. Follow manufacturer's instructions and use hot-iron transfer pencil to transfer one word pattern to each cream rectangle.

3. Refer to **Hand Stitches**, pg. 127, to Stem Stitch words.

4. Centering word, trim each "word" rectangle to 1 3/4"w and 1/2" longer than length of word.

5. Sew 1 plaid strip to each short side of each "word" rectangle. Staggering placement of "word" rectangle as desired, sew strips together along long sides. Trim sides of design to form a 7 1/2" square.

6. Cut doilies in half. Matching raw edges and centering 1 doily piece along 1 long edge of 1 side border, sew side border to center square. Whipstitch loose edge of doily in place. Repeat for remaining side border.

7. Sew 1 corner square to each end of remaining borders. Matching raw edges and centering 1 doily piece along 1 long edge of 1 border, sew top border to center square. Whipstitch loose edge of doily in place. Repeat for bottom border.

8. Sew buttons to centers of corner squares. Sew buttons to doilies. For each "o", sew button to each "word" rectangle.

9. Cut 4 12 1/2" lengths of rick rack. Centering rick rack along 1/4" seamline, baste 1 length to each edge of pillow top.

10. Refer to **Pillow Finishing**, pg. 127, to complete knife-edge pillow.

LIBERTY POUCH

(shown on pg. 40)

Finished Size: 6 1/2" X 9"

FABRICS

Yardage is based on 45"w fabric.
- blue solid — 3/8-yd
- ticking stripe — 3/8-yd
- red, blue, cream, and gold wool — scraps

Other Supplies
- buttons — one 3/8", two 9/16", one 11/16", and one 1 1/8"
- embroidery floss — black, cream, gold, and navy
- tracing paper
- sew-on Velcro® dot closure

CUTTING

All measurements include a 1/4" seam allowance.

Blue Solid:
- For pouch front, cut 1 rectangle 7" x 9".
- For pouch back, cut 1 rectangle 7" x 16".
- For strap, cut 2 strips 2" x 27" (pieced if necessary).

Ticking Stripe:
- For lining front, cut 1 rectangle 7" x 9".
- For lining back, cut 1 rectangle 7" x 16".
- For inside pocket, cut 1 rectangle 7" x 7".
- For outside pocket, cut 2 rectangles 3 3/4" x 5 1/4".
- For binding, cut 1 strip 1" x 25 1/2".

Red wool:
- Cut 3 stripes 1/2" x 4 3/4".

109

Blue wool:
• Cut 1 piece 1½" x 3¼".
Cream wool:
• Cut 4 stripes ½" x 4¾".
Gold wool:
• Use patterns to cut 2 stars.

INSTRUCTIONS

Use 2 strands of floss for all embroidery.

1. Fold tracing paper in half. Placing folded edge of tracing paper along dashed line of pattern, trace Flap pattern. Remove tracing paper from pattern. Turn traced pattern over. Trace drawn line on other side of tracing paper; open. Placing rounded end of pattern on 1 short side, use pattern to cut flap on pouch back and lining back.

2. For inside pocket, press 1 side ¼" to wrong side; press ¼" to wrong side again. Sew along folded edge.

3. Refer to **Hand Stitches**, pg. 127, to Blanket Stitch star to 1 outside pocket piece using gold floss.

4. For outside pocket, match right sides and raw edges and sew around all sides, leaving opening for turning; turn. Press and sew opening closed.

5. With top of pocket 1" from 1 short edge and with pocket centered, topstitch outside pocket to pouch front. Sew loop side of Velcro® closure 1¼" below pocket.

6. For pouch, match right sides and raw edges and sew pouch front to pouch back along 3 straight sides; turn.

7. Blanket Stitch red stripes to flap of pouch using black floss. Blanket Stitch cream stripes to flap using cream thread. Blanket Stitch blue piece to flap using black floss. Blanket Stitch gold star to flap using gold floss.

8. Use blue floss to Feather Stitch a line above and below flag. Nesting buttons, sew ⅜", ¹¹⁄₁₆", and 1⅛" buttons to point of flap.

9. For strap, sew short ends together. Press long edges of strip ½" to wrong side. Press strip in half lengthwise. Topstitch along folded edges. Press raw edges under. Sew ends to pouch back piece approximately ¼" below fold of flap. Sew remaining buttons over ends of strap.

10. For lining, with raw edges of inside pocket sandwiched in between, match right sides and raw edges of lining front and back and sew 3 straight sides together. Do **not** turn. Sew hook side of Velcro® closure ¾" below point of lining back.

11. Place lining inside pouch. Matching raw edges, baste around top of pouch.

12. Sew short ends of binding together. Press 1 long edge ¼" to wrong side. Matching raw edges, sew binding to pouch opening. Fold binding to inside; whipstitch in place over seamline.

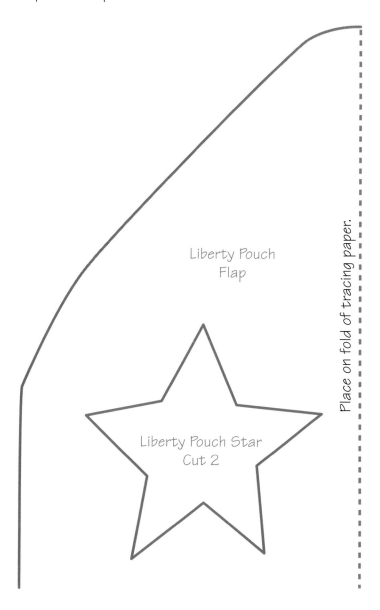

Liberty Pouch Flap

Liberty Pouch Star Cut 2

Place on fold of tracing paper.

BEE PROJECT KEEPER

(shown on pg. 40)

Finished Size: 10½" tall and 8" diameter

FABRICS

Yardage is based on 45"w fabric.
- black wool — ⅜-yd
- red wool — ¼-yd
- gold wool — ⅛-yd
- light gold wool — ⅛-yd
- dark green wool — ⅛-yd
- green wool — ⅛-yd
- small scrap of tan tweed
- green plaid flannel — ½-yd

Other Supplies
- embroidery floss — black and yellow
- paper-backed fusible web
- large safety pin

CUTTING

All measurements include a ½" seam allowance.

Black Wool:
- Cut 1 rectangle 25½" x 11" for bag sides.
- Use patterns, pg. 112, to cut:
  - 1 base.
  - 3 top bee stripes.
  - 3 bottom bee stripes.

Red Wool:
- Use pattern, pg. 112, to cut 5 flowers.

Gold Wool:
- Use pattern, pg. 112, to cut 5 flower bases.

Light Gold Wool:
- Use pattern, pg. 112 to cut 3 bees.

Dark Green Wool:
- Use pattern, pg. 112 to cut 5 stems.

Green Wool:
- Use pattern, pg. 112 to cut 5 leaves.

Tan Tweed:
- Use pattern, pg. 112, to cut 3 wings.

Green Plaid Flannel:
- Cut 1 rectangle 25½" x 11¾" for lining.
- Cut 1 base for lining.
- Cut 1 rectangle 2" x 24" for tie channel.
- Cut 1 rectangle 2½" x 42" for tie.

INSTRUCTIONS

1. Press long raw edges of tie channel ¼" to wrong side ¼"; press short ends 1" to wrong side.

2. Place channel 1½" from 1 long side (top). Topstitch along long edges of channel.

3. Follow **Preparing Appliqué Pieces**, pg. 119, and refer to **Appliqué Placement Diagram** to prepare and fuse appliqué pieces onto bag sides.

4. Refer to **Hand Stitches**, pg. 127, to Blanket stitch appliqués using 2 strands of black embroidery floss. Running Stitch "bee trail" using 2 strands of yellow embroidery floss.

5. With right sides together, use a ½" seam allowance to sew short ends of bag sides together to form a tube.

6. With right sides together, use a ½" seam allowance to sew black wool base to sides. Clip seam allowance as needed.

7. Repeat Steps 5 and 6 to make lining from green plaid flannel.

8. Press raw edge of lining ¼" to wrong side. Matching wrong sides, place lining into bag with side seams together. Fold the pressed edge of lining to outside to cover raw edge of bag. Topstitch lining to bag to form trim.

9. For tie, press long raw edges to wrong side ¼". Fold in half lengthwise and topstitch along folded edges. Pin large safety pin to one end of tie, and thread it through channel. Tie overhand knot at both ends of tie.

Appliqué Placement Diagram

Fold fabric in quarters. Place dashed lines of pattern on fold of fabric. Cut along solid line.

BEE NEEDLE CASE
(shown on pg. 40)

Finished Size: 5" square

FABRICS

Yardage is based on 45"w fabric.
- black wool — $^1/_4$-yd
- red wool — scrap
- gold plaid wool — scrap
- yellow wool — scrap
- green tweed — scrap
- green plaid — scrap
- dark green wool — scrap
- cotton fabric — $^1/_4$-yd

Other Supplies
- embroidery floss — black
- paper-backed fusible web
- $^5/_8$" diameter button

CUTTING
All measurements include a $^1/_4$" seam allowance.

Black Wool:
- Cut 1 rectangle $5^1/_2$" x $10^1/_2$" for front.
- Use pattern to cut closure.
- Use patterns to cut bee stripes.

Red Wool:
- Use pattern to cut flower.

Gold Plaid Wool:
• Use pattern to cut flower base.

Yellow Wool:
• Use pattern to cut bee.

Green Tweed:
• Use pattern to cut wings.

Green Plaid:
• Use pattern to cut 2 leaves.

Dark Green Wool:
• Use pattern to cut stem.
• Cut 1 rectangle 5¹/₂" x 2³/₄" for pocket.

Cotton Fabric:
• Cut 1 rectangle 5¹/₂" x 10¹/₂" for lining.

INSTRUCTIONS

1. Follow **Preparing Appliqué Pieces**, pg. 119, and refer to **Appliqué Placement Diagram**, to prepare and fuse appliqué pieces to 1 end of front.

2. Refer to **Hand Stitches**, pg. 127, to Blanket stitch appliqués using 2 strands of black embroidery floss.

3. Blanket Stitch along 1 long edge of pocket. Matching short raw edges, baste wrong side of pocket to right side of lining.

4. Matching right sides, sew lining to front, leaving an opening for turning; turn. Sew opening closed. Blanket Stitch around all sides of needle case.

5. Sew button to front. Cut a small slit in end of closure to fit over button. Blanket Stitch along edges of slit. Blanket Stitch along edges of closure, securing approximately 1" of end of closure to front as you stitch.

Appliqué Placement Diagram

"FRIENDS" WALL HANGING

(shown on pg. 41)

Finished Size: 14¹/₂" X 17"

FABRICS

Yardage is based on 45"w fabric.
• cream solid— ³/₈-yd
• green polka dot— ¹/₄-yd
• green floral— ¹/₂-yd
• fabric for backing — ¹/₂-yd

Other Supplies
• embroidery floss — black, lavender, gold, green
• batting — 45" x 60"
• hot-iron transfer pen
• tracing paper

CUTTING

All measurements include a ¹/₄" seam allowance.

Cream Solid:
• Cut 1 rectangle 9¹/₂" x 12" for background.

Green Polka Dot
• Cut 2 2" x 12" side inner borders.
• 2" x 11¹/₂" top/bottom inner borders.

Green Floral
• Cut 2 3" x 14" side outer borders.
• Cut 2 3" x 15¹/₂" top/bottom outer borders.

Backing Fabric:
• Cut 1 piece 3" x 15¹/₂" for hanging sleeve.
• Cut 1 piece 18¹/₂" x 21" for backing.

INSTRUCTIONS

Use 3 strands of floss for all embroidery. Use ¹/₄" seam allowances for sewing.

1. Trace pattern, pg. 114, onto tracing paper. Follow manufacturer's instructions and use hot-iron transfer pencil to transfer design to background.

2. Refer to **Hand Stitches**, pg. 127, to Stem Stitch words and trellis using black floss. Stem Stitch stems and leaves using green floss. Stem Stitch flowers using lavender floss. Straight Stitch flower centers using gold floss.

3. Sew side, then top and bottom inner borders to background.

4. Sew side, then top and bottom outer borders to complete wall hanging top.

5. Layer backing (right side up), wall hanging top (right side down), then batting. Stitch all layers together ¹/₄" from outer edges leaving an opening for turning. Turn wall hanging right side out and slipstitch opening closed.

6. Use long quilting stitches and quilting thread to outline quilt ¹/₄" around outer edges of linen and polka dot fabric, and ¹/₂" from outer edge of wall hanging.

7. Steep 1 tea bag in 2 cups of hot water; allow to cool. Immerse wall hanging in tea. Soak until desired color is achieved. Remove from tea and allow to dry. Press if desired.

QUILTER'S BASICS

All yardage amounts listed are based on 45"w 100% cotton fabric with a "usable width" of 42" after washing and trimming selvages. When sewing, match right sides and raw edges and use an accurate ¼" seam allowance unless otherwise specified.

BASIC TOOLS
ROTARY CUTTING:
18" x 24" rotary cutting mat
6" x 24" rotary cutting ruler with 45° marking
rotary cutter – 45mm size
right-angle triangle

MACHINE-PIECING:
sewing machine
straight pins
scissors
all-purpose sewing thread in neutral color
seam ripper

PRESSING:
steam iron

APPLIQUÉING:
template plastic
hand-sewing needles – sharps
all-purpose sewing thread to match
each appliqué fabric

HAND QUILTING:
Quilting needles – betweens
Quilting thread
Quilting hoop or frame

MACHING QUILTING:
large brass safety pins
walking foot or even-feed foot for
sewing machine

ROTARY CUTTING

Observe safety precautions when using the rotary cutter since it is extremely sharp. Develop a habit of retracting the blade guard just before making a cut and closing it immediately afterward, before laying down the cutter.

1. Wash, dry, and press fabrics.

2. Refold each piece of fabric lengthwise (as it was on the bolt) with wrong sides together and matching selvages. If necessary adjust fabric slightly at selvages so that fold lies flat; press.

3. Cut all strips from the selvage-to-selvage width of the fabric unless otherwise indicated in project instructions. Place fabric on the cutting mat with the fold of the fabric toward you (Fig. 1). To straighten the uneven fabric edge, make the first "squaring up" cut by placing the right edge of the rotary cutting ruler over the left raw edge of the fabric. Place right-angle triangle (or another rotary cutting ruler) with the lower edge carefully aligned with the fold and the left edge against the ruler (Fig. 1). Hold the ruler firmly with your left hand, placing your little finger off the left edge to anchor the ruler. Remove the triangle, pick up the rotary cutter, and retract the blade guard. Using a smooth downward motion, make the cut by running the blade of the rotary cutter firmly along the right edge of the ruler (Fig. 2). Always cut in a direction away from your body and immediately close the blade guard after each cut.

Fig. 1

Fig. 2

4. To cut each of the strips required for a project, place the ruler over the cut edge of the fabric, aligning desired marking on the ruler with the cut edge (Fig. 3); make the cut. When cutting several strips from a single piece of fabric, check frequently that cuts remain at a perfect right angle to the fold.

Fig. 3

5. To square up selvage ends of a strip before cutting pieces, refer to Fig. 4 and place folded strip on a mat with selvage ends to your right. Aligning a horizontal marking on ruler with 1 long edge of strip, then trim selvage to make end of strip square and even (Fig. 4). Turn strip (or entire mat) so that cut end is to your left before making further cuts.

Fig. 4

6. Pieces such as rectangles and squares can now be cut from strips. Usually strips remain folded, and pieces are cut in pairs after ends of strips are squared up. To cut squares or rectangles from a strip, place ruler over left end of strip, aligning desired marking on ruler with cut end of strip. To ensure perfectly square cuts, align a horizontal marking on ruler with 1 long edge of strip (Fig. 5) before making the cut.

Fig. 5

7. To cut 2 triangles from a square, cut square the size indicated in the project instructions. Cut square once diagonally to make 2 triangles (Fig. 6).

Fig. 6

8. To cut 4 triangles from a square, cut square the size indicated in the project instructions. Cut square twice diagonally to make 4 triangles (Fig. 7).

Fig. 7

9. In some cases, strips will be sewn together into strip sets before being cut into smaller units. When cutting a strip set, align a seam in strip set with a horizontal marking on the ruler to maintain square cuts (Fig. 8).

Fig. 8

TEMPLATE CUTTING

Our full-sized piecing template patterns have 2 lines — a solid cutting line and a dashed line showing the ¹/₄" seam allowance. Patterns for appliqué templates do not include seam allowances.

1. To make a template from a pattern, use a permanent fine-point pen to carefully trace pattern onto template plastic, making sure to transfer all alignment and grain line markings. Cut out template along inner edge of drawn line. Check template against original pattern for accuracy.

2. To use a template, place template on wrong side of fabric (unless otherwise indicated in project instructions), aligning grain line on template with straight grain of fabric. Use a sharp fabric-marking pencil to draw around template. Transfer all alignment markings to fabric. Cut out fabric piece using scissors or rotary cutting equipment.

PIECING

Set sewing machine stitch length for approximately 11 stitches per inch. Use a new, sharp needle suited for medium-weight woven fabric. Use a neutral-colored general-purpose sewing thread (not quilting thread) in the needle and in the bobbin.

Using an accurate ¹/₄" seam allowance is essential. On many sewing machines, the measurement from the needle to the outer edge of the presser foot is ¹/₄". If this is not the case with your machine, measure ¹/₄" from the needle and mark throat plate with a piece of masking tape. Special presser feet that are exactly ¹/₄" wide are also available for most sewing machines.

When piecing, always place pieces right sides together and match raw edges; pin if necessary.

SEWING STRIP SETS

When sewing several strips into a strip set, first sew the strips together into pairs, then sew the pairs together to form the strip set. To help avoid distortion, sew 1 seam in 1 direction and then sew the next seam in the opposite direction (Fig. 9).

Fig. 9

SEWING ACROSS SEAM INTERSECTIONS

When sewing across the intersection of 2 seams, place pieces right sides together and match seams exactly, making sure seam allowances are pressed in opposite directions (Fig. 10).

Fig. 10

SEWING BIAS SEAMS

Care should be used in handling and stitching bias edges since they stretch easily. After sewing the seam, carefully press seam allowance to 1 side, making sure not to stretch fabric.

SEWING SHARP POINTS

To ensure sharp points when joining triangular or diagonal pieces, stitch across the center of the "X" (shown in pink) formed on the wrong side by previous seams (Fig. 11).

Fig. 11

MAKING TRIANGLE-SQUARES

The grid method for making triangle-squares is faster and more accurate than cutting and sewing individual triangles. Stitching before cutting the triangle-squares apart also prevents stretching the bias edges.

1. Follow project instructions to cut rectangles or squares of fabric for making triangle-squares. Place the indicated pieces right sides together and press.

2. On the wrong side of the lighter fabric, draw a grid of squares similar to that shown in Fig. 12. The size and number of squares will be given in the project instructions. Following the example given in the project instructions, draw 1 diagonal line through each square in the grid (Fig. 13).

Fig. 12   Fig. 13

3. Stitch ¼" on each side of all diagonal lines, drawing stitching lines ahead of time if needed. Project instructions include a diagram similar to Fig. 14, which shows stitching lines and the direction of the stitching.

Fig. 14

4. Cut along all drawn lines of the grid. Each square of the grid will yield 2 triangle-squares (Fig. 15).

Fig. 15

5. Carefully press triangle-squares open, pressing seam allowances toward darker fabric.

TRIMMING SEAM ALLOWANCES

When sewing with diamond or triangle pieces, some seam allowances may extend beyond the edges of the sewn pieces. Trim away "dog ears" that extend beyond the edges of the sewn pieces (Fig. 16).

Fig. 16

← Trim points

PRESSING

Use a steam iron set on "Cotton" for all pressing. Press as you sew, taking care to prevent small folds along seamlines. Seam allowances are usually pressed to one side, usually toward the darker fabric. However, to reduce bulk it may occasionally be necessary to press seam allowances toward the lighter fabric or even to press them open. To prevent a dark fabric seam allowance from showing through a light fabric, trim the darker seam allowance slightly narrower than the lighter seam allowance. To press long seams, such as those in long strip sets, without curving or other distortion, lay strips across the width of the ironing board.

FOUNDATION PIECING

PREPARING YOUR SEWING MACHINE

1. To prepare your sewing machine for foundation piecing, insert a 90/14 needle. This needle will help perforate your paper to make the needle-punch foundations. This needle should then be reserved exclusively for the use on foundation work, as paper will dull needles quickly.

2. Set your machine to a short straight stitch (18 stitches per inch). It is helpful to use an open-toe foot.

MAKING NEEDLE-PUNCH PAPER FOUNDATIONS

1. Using a fine-point marker and leaving at least a 1" space around design, trace desired pattern.

2. To make needle-punch foundations, place up to eight pieces of foundation paper (notebook paper will do) under traced pattern and secure with pins. With your needle in your machine but no thread, sew precisely on the drawn lines. The punched holes serve as your sewing guide.

3. Cut out leaving at least 1" around the design.

PIECING

1. Place your original pattern nearby as a guide. If you wish, transfer numbers to your needle-punched foundations.

2. Thread your machine with a neutral-colored thread. Follow project instructions to place and sew fabric.

3. Rough cut a piece of fabric at least ¹⁄₂" larger on all sides than area 1 on the foundation.

4. Center fabric piece right side up on back of foundation; completely cover area 1 with fabric.

5. Fold foundation on line between area 1 and area 2. Trim fabric ¹⁄₄" from fold (Fig. 17). Unfold foundation.

Fig. 17

6. Rough cut a piece of fabric in the same manner for area 2 on foundation. Matching trimmed edge, place piece #2 right sides together on piece #1, making sure fabric extends beyond outer seamlines (Fig. 18). Turn foundation over to front and pin.

Fig. 18

7. Sew along punched line between areas 1 and 2, extending sewing a few stitches beyond beginning and end of line (Fig. 19).

Fig. 19

8. Open out piece #2; press. Pin piece #2 to foundation (Fig. 20).

Fig. 20

9. Repeat adding pieces in same manner until foundation is covered.

10. Trim fabric and foundation ¹⁄₄" outside punched lines.

11. When removing paper from fabric, score the seams with the eye of a large needle or use tweezers to gently remove small pieces.

APPLIQUÉ

PREPARING APPLIQUÉ PIECES

Patterns are printed in reverse to enable you to use our speedy method of preparing appliqués. This method can be used when securing appliqués with Invisible Appliqué, Satin Stitch Appliqué, or Mock Hand Appliqué. White or light-colored fabrics may need to be lined with fusible interfacing before applying fusible web to prevent darker fabrics from showing through.

1. Place paper-backed fusible web, web side down, over appliqué pattern. Use a pencil to trace pattern onto paper side of web as many times as indicated in project instructions for a single fabric. Repeat for additional patterns and fabrics.

2. Follow manufacturer's instructions to fuse traced patterns to wrong side of fabrics. Do not remove paper backing. (Note: Some pieces may be given as measurements, such as a 2" x 4" rectangle, instead of drawn patterns. Fuse web to wrong side of the fabrics indicated for these pieces.)

3. Use scissors to cut out appliqué pieces along traced lines; use rotary cutting equipment to cut out appliqué pieces given as measurements. Remove paper backing from all pieces.

INVISIBLE APPLIQUÉ

This machine appliqué method uses clear nylon thread to secure the appliqué pieces. Transparent monofilament (clear nylon) thread is available in 2 colors: clear and smoke. Use clear on white or very light fabrics and smoke on darker colors.

1. Referring to diagram and/or photo, arrange prepared appliqués on the background fabric and follow manufacturer's instructions to fuse in place.

2. Pin a stabilizer, such as paper or any of the commercially available products, on wrong side of background fabric before stitching appliqués in place.

3. Thread sewing machine with transparent monofilament thread; use general-purpose thread that matches background fabric in bobbin.

4. Set sewing machine for a very narrow width (approximately 1/16") zigzag stitch and a short stitch length. You may find that loosening the top tension slightly will yield a smoother stitch.

5. Begin by stitching 2 or 3 stitches in place (drop feed dogs or set stitch length at 0) to anchor thread. Most of the zigzag stitch should be done on the appliqué with the right edges of the stitch falling at the very outside edge of the appliqué. Stitch over all exposed raw edges of appliqué pieces.

6. (Note: Dots on Figs. 21-26 indicate where to leave needle in fabric when pivoting.) For outside corners, stitch just past the corner, stopping with the needle in background fabric (Fig. 21). Raise presser foot. Pivot project, lower presser foot, and stitch adjacent side (Fig. 22).

Fig. 21   Fig. 22

7. For **inside corners**, stitch just past the corner, stopping with the needle in **appliqué** fabric (Fig. 23). Raise presser foot. Pivot project, lower presser foot, and stitch adjacent side (Fig. 24).

Fig. 23   Fig. 24

8. When stitching **outside** curves, stop with needle in **background** fabric. Raise presser foot and pivot project as needed. Lower presser foot and continue stitching, pivoting as often as necessary to follow curve (Fig. 25).

Fig. 25

9. When stitching **inside** curves, stop with needle in **appliqué** fabric. Raise presser foot and pivot project as needed. Lower presser foot and continue stitching, pivoting as often as necessary to follow curve (Fig. 26).

Fig. 26

10. Do not backstitch at end of stitching. Pull threads to wrong side of background fabric; knot thread and trim ends.

11. Carefully tear away stabilizer.

NEEDLE-TURN APPLIQUÉ

In this traditional hand appliqué method, the needle is used to turn the seam allowance under as you sew the appliqué to the background fabric using a Blind Stitch, page 127. When stitching, match the color of thread to the color of appliqué to disguise your stitches. Appliqué each piece starting with the ones directly on the background fabric. It is not necessary to appliqué areas that will be covered by another appliqué. Stitches on the right side of fabric should not show. Stitches on the edge of an appliqué and on background fabric should be equal in length. Clipped areas should be secured with a few extra stitches to prevent fraying.

1. Follow **Template Cutting**, pg. 116, Step 1 to cut templates from template plastic.

2. Place template on right side of appliqué fabric. Use a pencil to lightly draw around template, leaving at least ¹/₂" between shapes; repeat for number of shapes specified in project instructions.

3. Cut out shapes approximately ³/₁₆" outside drawn line. Clip inside curves and points up to, but not through, drawn line. Arrange shapes on background fabric and pin or baste in place.

4. Thread a sharps needle with a single strand of general-purpose sewing thread; knot one end.

5. Pin center of appliqué to right side of background fabric. Begin on as straight an edge as possible and use point of needle to turn under a small amount of seam allowance, concealing drawn line on appliqué. Hold seam allowance in place with thumb of your non-sewing hand (Fig. 27).

Fig. 27

6. To stitch, bring needle up through background fabric at 1, even with turned edge of appliqué (Fig. 28).

Fig. 28

7. Insert needle into turned edge at 2, directly across from 1. Bring needle out of folded edge at 3 (Fig. 29). Insert needle into background fabric at 4, even with edge of appliqué and directly across from 3. Bring needle up through background fabric at 5, forming a small stitch on wrong side of fabric (Fig. 30).

Fig. 29   Fig. 30

8. Continue needle-turning method to completely secure appliqué, referring to information below about stitching outward points and bias strips.

Stitching Outward Points: Appliqué long edge of shape until you are about ¹/₂" from the point (Fig. 31). Turn seam allowance under at point (Fig. 32). Turn remainder of seam allowance between stitching and point, using non-stitching thumb to hold allowance in place. Stitch to point, taking 2 or 3 stitches at top of point to secure. Turn under small amount of seam allowance past point and resume stitching.

Fig. 31   Fig. 32

Stitching Pressed Bias Strips: Since seam allowances have already been stitched or pressed under during preparation of bias strips used as appliqués, simply baste bias strip to background fabric, then stitch in place along edges using the same blindstitch used in needle-turning.

SATIN STITCH APPLIQUÉ

A good satin stitch is a thick, smooth, almost solid line of zigzag stitching that covers the exposed raw edges of appliqué pieces.

1. Place a stabilizer, such as paper or any of the commercially available products, on wrong side of background fabric before stitching appliqués in place.

2. Thread needle of sewing machine with general-purpose thread. Use thread that matches the background fabric in the bobbin for all stitching. Set sewing machine for a medium width zigzag stitch (approximately 1/8") and a very short stitch length. Set upper tension slightly looser than for regular stitching.

3. Beginning on as straight an edge as possible, position fabric so that most of the satin stitch will be on the appliqué piece. Do not backstitch; hold upper thread toward you and sew over it two or three stitches to anchor thread. Following Steps 6–9 of **Invisible Appliqué,** pg. 119, for stitching corners and curves, stitch over exposed raw edges of appliqué pieces, changing thread color as necessary.

4. Do not backstitch at end of stitching. Pull threads to wrong side of background fabric; knot thread and trim ends. Remove paper and stabilizer.

MOCK HAND APPLIQUÉ

This technique uses the blindstitch on your sewing machine to achieve a look that closely resembles traditional hand appliqué. Using an updated method, appliqués are prepared with turned-under edges and then machine stitched to the background fabric. For best appliqué results, your sewing machine must have blindstitch capability with a variable stitch width. If your blindstitch width cannot be adjusted, you may still wish to try this technique to see if you are happy with the results. Some sewing machines have a narrower blindstitch width than others.

1. Follow project instructions to prepare appliqué pieces.

2. Thread needle of sewing machine with transparent monofilament thread; use general-purpose thread in bobbin in a color to match background fabric.

3. Set sewing machine for narrow blindstitch (just wide enough to catch 2 or 3 threads of the appliqué) and a very short stitch length (20 - 30 stitches per inch).

4. Arrange appliqué pieces on background fabric as described in project instructions. Use pins or hand baste to secure.

5. (Note: Follow Steps 6 - 9 of **Invisible Appliqué,** page 119, for needle position when pivoting.) Sew around edges of each appliqué so that the straight stitches fall on the background fabric very near the appliqué and the "hem" stitches barely catch the folded edge of the appliqué (Fig. 33)

Fig. 33

6. It is not necessary to backstitch at the beginning or end of stitching. End stitching by sewing 1/4" over the first stitches. Trim thread ends close the fabric.

BORDERS

Borders cut along the lengthwise grain will lie flatter than borders cut along the crosswise grain. In most cases, our instructions for cutting borders for bed-size quilts include an extra 2" of length at each end for "insurance"; borders will be trimmed after measuring completed center section of quilt top.

ADDING SQUARED BORDERS

1. Mark the center of each edge of quilt top.

2. Our borders are most often added to the side edges, then the top and bottom edges of a quilt top. To add side borders, measure center of quilt top to determine length of borders (Fig. 34). Trim side borders to the determined length.

Fig. 34

3. Mark center of 1 long edge of side border. Matching center marks and raw edges, pin border to quilt top, easing in any fullness; stitch. Repeat for remaining side border.

4. Measure center of quilt top, including attached borders, to determine length of top and bottom borders. Trim borders to the determined length. Repeat Step 3 to add borders to quilt top (Fig. 35).

Fig. 35

ADDING MITERED BORDERS

1. Mark the center of each edge of quilt top.

2. Mark center of 1 long edge of top border. Measure across center of quilt top (see Fig. 34). Matching center marks and raw edges, pin border to center of quilt top edge. Beginning at center of border, measure $1/2$ the width of the quilt top in both directions and mark. Match marks on border with corners of quilt top and pin. Easing in any fullness, pin border to quilt top between center and corners. Sew border to quilt top, beginning and ending seams exactly $1/4$" from each corner of quilt top and backstitching at beginning and end of stitching (Fig. 36).

Fig. 36

3. Repeat Step 2 to sew bottom, then side borders, to center section of quilt top. To temporarily move first 2 borders out of the way, fold and pin ends as shown in Fig. 37.

Fig. 37

4. Fold 1 corner of quilt top diagonally with right sides together and matching edges. Use ruler to mark stitching line as shown in Fig. 38. Pin borders together along drawn line. Sew on drawn line, backstitching at beginning and end of stitching (Fig. 39).

Fig. 38   Fig. 39

5. Turn mitered corner right side up. Check to make sure corner will lie flat with no gaps or puckers.

6. Trim seam allowances to $1/4$"; press to 1 side.

7. Repeat Steps 4 - 6 to miter each remaining corner.

QUILTING

Quilting holds the 3 layers (top, batting, and backing) of the quilt together and can be done by hand or machine. Our project instructions tell you which method is used on each project. Because marking, layering, and quilting are interrelated and may be done in different orders depending on circumstances, please read the entire **Quilting** section, pages 123 - 124, before beginning the quilting process on your project.

TYPES OF QUILTING
In-The-Ditch-Quilting

Quilting very close to a seamline or appliqué is called "in-the-ditch" quilting. This type of quilting does not need to be marked. When quilting in the ditch, quilt on the side **opposite** the seam allowance.

Outline Quilting

Quilting approximately $1/4$" from a seam or appliqué is called "outline" quilting. Outline quilting may be marked, or you may place $1/4$"w masking tape along seamlines and quilt along the opposite edge of the tape. (Do not leave tape on quilt longer than necessary, since it may leave an adhesive residue.)

Ornamental Quilting

Quilting decorative lines or designs is called "ornamental" quilting. This type of quilting should be marked before you baste quilt layers together.

MARKING QUILTING LINES

Fabric marking pencils, various types of chalk markers, and fabric marking pens with inks that disappear with exposure to air or water are readily available and work well for different applications. Lead pencils work well on light-color fabrics, but marks may be difficult to remove. White pencils work well on dark-color fabrics, and silver pencils show up well on many colors. Since chalk rubs off easily, it's a good choice if you are marking as you quilt. Fabric marking pens make more durable and visible markings, but the marks should be carefully removed according to manufacturer's instructions. Press down only as hard as necessary to make a visible line.

When you choose to mark your quilt, whether before or after the layers are basted together, is also a factor in deciding which marking tool to use. If you mark with chalk or a chalk pencil, handling the quilt during basting may rub off the markings. Intricate or ornamental designs may not be practical to mark as you quilt; mark these designs before basting using a more durable marker.

To choose marking tools, take all these factors into consideration and **test** different markers **on scrap fabric** until you find the one that gives the desired result.

CHOOSING AND PREPARING THE BACKING

To allow for slight shifting of the quilt top during quilting, the backing should be approximately 4" larger on all sides for a bed-size quilt top or approximately 2" larger on all sides for a wall hanging. Yardage requirements listed for quilt backings are calculated for 45"w fabric. If you are making a bed-size quilt, using 90"w or 108"w fabric for the backing may eliminate piecing. To piece a backing using 45"w fabric, use the following instructions.

1. Measure length and width of quilt top; add 8" (4" for a wall hanging) to each measurement.

2. If quilt top is 76"w or less, cut backing fabric into 2 lengths slightly longer than the determined length measurement. Trim selvages. Place lengths with right sides facing and sew long edges together, forming a tube (Fig. 40). Match seams and press along 1 fold (Fig. 41). Cut along pressed fold to form a single piece (Fig. 42).

Fig. 40   Fig. 41   Fig. 42

3. If quilt top is more than 76"w, cut backing fabric into 3 lengths slightly longer than the determined width measurement. Trim selvages. Sew long edges together to form a single piece.

4. Trim backing to correct size, if necessary, and press seam allowances open.

CHOOSING AND PREPARING THE BATTING

Choosing the right batting will make your quilting job easier. For fine hand quilting, choose a low-loft batting in any of the fiber types described here. Machine quilters will want to choose a low-loft batting that is all cotton or a cotton/polyester blend because the cotton helps "grip" the layers of the quilt. If the quilt is to be tied, a high-loft batting, sometimes called extra-loft or fat batting, is a good choice.

Batting is available in many different fibers. Bonded polyester batting is one of the most popular batting types. It is treated with a protective coating to stabilize the fibers and to reduce "bearding," a process in which batting fibers work their way out through the quilt fabrics. Other batting options include cotton/polyester batting, which combines the best of both polyester and cotton battings; all-cotton batting, which must be quilted more closely than polyester batting; and wool and silk battings, which are generally more expensive and usually only dry-cleanable.

Whichever batting you choose, read the manufacturer's instructions closely for any special notes on care or preparation. When you're ready to use your chosen batting in a project, cut batting the same size as the prepared backing.

ASSEMBLING THE QUILT

1. Examine wrong side of quilt top closely; trim any seam allowances and clip any threads that may show through the front of the quilt. Press quilt top.

2. If quilt top is to be marked before layering, mark quilting lines (see Marking Quilting Lines).

3. Place backing **wrong** side up on a flat surface. Use masking tape to tape edges of backing to surface. Place batting on top of backing fabric. Smooth batting gently, being careful not to stretch or tear. Center quilt top **right** side up on batting.

4. If hand quilting, begin in the center and work toward the outer edges to hand baste all layers together. Use long stitches and place basting lines approximately 4" apart (Fig. 43). Smooth fullness or wrinkles toward outer edges.

Fig. 43

5. If machine quilting, use 1" rustproof safety pins to "pin-baste" all layers together, spacing pins approximately 4" apart. Begin at the center and work toward the outer edges to secure all layers. If possible, place pins away from areas that will be quilted, although pins may be removed as needed when quilting.

HAND QUILTING

The quilting stitch is a basic running stitch that forms a broken line on the quilt top and backing. Stitches on the quilt top and backing should be straight and equal in length.

1. Secure center of quilt in hoop or frame. Check quilt top and backing to make sure they are smooth. To help prevent puckers, always begin quilting in the center of the quilt and work toward the outside edges.

2. Thread needle with an 18" - 20" length of quilting thread; knot 1 end. Using a thimble, insert needle into quilt top and batting approximately 1/2" from where you wish to begin quilting. Bring needle up at the point where you wish to begin (Fig. 44); when knot catches on quilt top, give thread a quick, short pull to "pop" knot through fabric into batting (Fig. 45).

Fig. 44

Fig. 45

3. Holding the needle with your sewing hand and placing your other hand underneath the quilt, use thimble to push the tip of the needle down through all layers. As soon as needle touches your finger underneath, use that finger to push the tip of the needle only back up through the layers to top of quilt. (The amount of the needle showing above the fabric determines the length of the quilting stitch.) Referring to Fig. 46, rock the needle up and down, taking 3 - 6 stitches before bringing the needle and thread completely through the layers. Check the back of the quilt to make sure stitches are going through all layers. When quilting through a seam allowance or quilting a curve or corner, you may need to make 1 stitch at a time.

Fig. 46

4. When you reach the end of your thread, knot thread close to the fabric and "pop" knot into batting; clip thread close to fabric.

5. Stop and move your hoop as often as necessary. You do not have to tie a knot every time you move your hoop; you may leave the thread dangling and pick it up again when you return to that part of the quilt.

MACHINE QUILTING

The following instructions are for straight-line quilting, which requires a walking foot or even-feed foot. The term "straight-line" is somewhat deceptive, since curves (especially gentle ones) as well as straight lines can be stitched with this technique.

1. Wind your sewing machine bobbin with general-purpose thread that matches the quilt backing. Do not use quilting thread. Thread the needle of your machine with transparent monofilament thread if you want your quilting to blend with your quilt top fabrics. Use decorative thread, such as a metallic or contrasting-color general-purpose thread, when you want the quilting lines to stand out more. Set the stitch length for 6 - 10 stitches per inch and attach the walking foot to sewing machine.

2. After pin-basting, decide which section of the quilt will have the longest continuous quilting line, oftentimes the area from center top to center bottom. Leaving the area exposed where you will place your first line of quilting, roll up each edge of the quilt to help reduce the bulk, keeping fabrics smooth. Smaller projects may not need to be rolled.

3. Start stitching at beginning of longest quilting line, using very short stitches for the first 1/4" to "lock" beginning of quilting line. Stitch across project, using one hand on each side of the walking foot to slightly spread the fabric and to guide the fabric through the machine. Lock stitches at end of quilting line.

4. Continue machine quilting, stitching longer quilting lines first to stabilize the quilt before moving on to other areas.

BINDING

Binding encloses the raw edges of your quilt. Because of its stretchiness, bias binding works well for binding projects with curves or rounded corners and tends to lie smooth and flat in any given circumstance. It is also more durable than other types of binding. Binding may also be cut from the straight lengthwise or crosswise grain of the fabric. You will find that straight-grain binding works well for projects with straight edges.

MAKING CONTINUOUS BIAS STRIP BINDING

Bias strips for binding can simply be cut and pieced to the desired length. However, when a long length of binding is needed, the "continuous" method is quick and accurate.

1. Cut a square from binding fabric the size indicated in the project instructions. Cut square in half diagonally to make 2 triangles.

2. With right sides together and using a 1/4" seam allowance, sew triangles together (Fig. 47); press seam allowance open.

Fig. 47

3. On wrong side of fabric, draw lines the width of the binding as specified in the project instructions, usually 2¹/₂" (Fig. 48). Cut off any remaining fabric less than this width.

Fig. 48

4. With right sides inside, bring short edges together to form a tube; match raw edges so that first drawn line of top section meets second drawn line of bottom section (Fig. 49).

Fig. 49

5. Carefully pin edges together by inserting pins through drawn lines at the point where drawn lines intersect, making sure the pins go through intersections on both sides. Using a ¹/₄" seam allowance, sew edges together. Press seam allowance open.

6. To cut continuous strip, begin cutting along first drawn line (Fig. 50). Continue cutting along drawn line around tube.

Fig. 50

7. Trim ends of bias strip square.

8. Matching wrong sides and raw edges, press bias strip in half lengthwise to complete binding.

MAKING STRAIGHT-GRAIN BINDING

1. To determine length of strip needed if attaching binding with mitered corners, measure edges of the quilt and add 12".

2. To determine lengths of strips needed if attaching binding with overlapped corners, measure each edge of quilt; add 3" to each measurement.

3. Cut lengthwise or crosswise strips of binding fabric the determined length and the width called for in the project instructions. Strips may be pieced to achieve the necessary length.

4. Matching wrong sides and raw edges, press strip(s) in half lengthwise to complete binding.

ATTACHING BINDING WITH MITERED CORNERS

1. Press 1 end of binding diagonally (Fig. 51).

Fig. 51

2. Beginning with pressed end several inches from a corner, lay binding around quilt to make sure that seams in binding will not end up at a corner. Adjust placement if necessary. Matching raw edges of binding to raw edge of quilt top, pin binding to right side of quilt along 1 edge.

3. When you reach the first corner, mark ¹/₄" from corner of quilt top (Fig. 52).

Fig. 52

4. Using a ¹/₄" seam allowance, sew binding to quilt, backstitching at beginning of stitching and when you reach the mark (Fig. 53). Lift needle out of fabric and clip thread.

Fig. 53

5. Fold binding as shown in Figs. 54 and 55 and pin binding to adjacent side, matching raw edges. When you reach the next corner, mark ¹/₄" from edge of quilt top.

Fig. 54   Fig. 55

6. Backstitching at edge of quilt top, sew pinned binding to quilt (Fig. 56); backstitch when you reach the next mark. Lift needle out of fabric and clip thread.

Fig. 56

7. Repeat Steps 5 and 6 to continue sewing binding to quilt until binding overlaps beginning end by approximately 2". Trim excess binding.

8. If using 2¹/₂"w binding (finished size ¹/₂"), trim backing and batting a scant ¹/₄" larger than quilt top so that batting and backing will fill the binding when it is folded over to the quilt backing. If using narrower binding, trim backing and batting even with edges of quilt top.

9. On 1 edge of quilt, fold binding over to quilt backing and pin pressed edge in place, covering stitching line (Fig. 57). On adjacent side, fold binding over, forming a mitered corner (Fig. 58). Repeat to pin remainder of binding in place.

Fig. 57

Fig. 58

10. Follow **Hand Stitches**, to Blindstitch binding to backing, taking care not to stitch through to front of quilt.

ATTACHING BINDING WITH OVERLAPPED CORNERS

1. Matching raw edges and using a ¹/₄" seam allowance, sew a length of binding to top and bottom edges on right side of quilt.

2. If using 2¹/₂"w binding (finished size ¹/₂"), trim backing and batting from top and bottom edges a scant ¹/₄" larger than quilt top so that batting and backing will fill the binding when it is folded over to the quilt backing. If using narrower binding, trim backing and batting even with edges of quilt top.

3. Trim ends of top and bottom binding even with edges of quilt top. Fold binding over to quilt backing and pin pressed edges in place, covering stitching line (Fig. 59); blindstitch binding to backing.

Fig. 59

4. Leaving approximately 1¹/₂" of binding at each end, stitch a length of binding to each side edge of quilt. Trim backing and batting as in Step 2.

5. Trim each end of binding ¹/₂" longer than bound edge. Fold each end of binding over to quilt backing (Fig. 60); pin in place. Fold binding over to quilt backing and blindstitch in place, taking care not to stitch through to front of quilt.

Fig. 60

MAKING A HANGING SLEEVE

Attaching a hanging sleeve to the back of your wall hanging or quilt before the binding is added allows you to display your completed project on a wall.

1. Measure the width of the wall hanging or quilt top and subtract 1". Cut a piece of fabric 7"w by the determined measurement.

2. Press short edges of fabric piece ¹/₄" to wrong side; press edges ¹/₄" to wrong side again and machine stitch in place.

3. Matching wrong sides, fold piece in half lengthwise to form a tube.

4. Follow project instructions to sew binding to quilt top and to trim backing and batting. Before blindstitching binding to backing, match raw edges and stitch hanging sleeve to center top edge on back of wall hanging.

5. Finish binding wall hanging, treating the hanging sleeve as part of the backing.

6. Blindstitch bottom of hanging sleeve to backing, taking care not to stitch through to front of quilt.

7. Insert dowel or slat into hanging sleeve.

PILLOW FINISHING

If desired, you may add welting and/or a ruffle to the pillow top before sewing the pillow top and back together.

ADDING WELTING TO PILLOW TOP

1. To make welting, use bias strip indicated in project instructions. (Or measure edges of pillow top and add 4". Measure circumference of cord and add 2". Cut a bias strip of fabric the determined measurement, piecing if necessary.)

2. Lay cord along center of bias strip on wrong side of fabric; fold strip over cord. Using a zipper foot, machine baste along length of strip close to cord. Trim seam allowance to the width you will use to sew pillow top and back together (see Step 2 of **Making A Knife-Edge Pillow**).

3. Matching raw edges and beginning and ending 3" from ends of welting, baste welting to right side of pillow top. To make turning corners easier, clip seam allowance of welting at pillow top corners.

4. Remove approximately 3" of seam at 1 end of welting; fold fabric away from cord. Trim remaining end of welting so that cord ends meet exactly (Fig. 61).

Fig. 61

5. Fold short edge of welting fabric 1/2" to wrong side; fold fabric back over area where ends meet (Fig. 62).

Fig. 62

6. Baste remainder of welting to pillow top close to cord (Fig. 63).

Fig. 63

7. Follow Making A Knife-Edge Pillow to complete pillow.

ADDING RUFFLE TO PILLOW TOP

1. To make ruffle, use fabric strip indicated in project instructions.

2. Matching right sides, use a 1/4" seam allowance to sew short edges of ruffle together to form a large circle; press seam allowance open. To form ruffle, fold along length with wrong sides together and raw edges matching; press.

3. To gather ruffle, place quilting thread 1/4" from raw edge of ruffle. Using a medium-width zigzag stitch with medium stitch length, stitch over quilting thread, being careful not to catch quilting thread in stitching. Pull quilting thread, drawing up gathers to fit pillow top.

4. Matching raw edges, baste ruffle to right side of pillow top.

5. Follow **Making A Knife-Edge Pillow** to complete pillow.

MAKING A KNIFE-EDGE PILLOW

1. For pillow back, cut a piece of fabric the same size as pillow top.

2. Place pillow back and pillow top right sides together. The seam allowance width you use will depend on the construction of the pillow top. If the pillow top has borders on which the finished width of the border is not crucial, use a 1/2" seam allowance for durability. If the pillow top is pieced so that a wider seam allowance would interfere with the design, use a 1/4" seam allowance. Using the determined seam allowance (or stitching as close as possible to welting), sew pillow top and back together, leaving an opening at bottom edge for turning.

3. Turn pillow right side out, carefully pushing corners outward. Stuff with polyester fiberfill or pillow form and sew final closure by hand.

HAND STITCHES

BLIND STITCH

SATIN STITCH

STEM STITCH

RUNNING STITCH

BLANKET STITCH

FEATHER STITCH

CHAIN STITCH

BACK STITCH

FRENCH KNOT

STRAIGHT STITCH

CROSS STITCH

Credits

We want to extend a warm thank you to Nancy Gunn Porter and Sandra Cook for allowing us to photograph some of our quilts at their homes.

We want to especially thank photographers Ken West and Mark Mathews of The Peerless Group, Jerry R. Davis of Jerry Davis Photography and Andrew Uilkie of Uilkie Photography, all of Little Rock, Arkansas, for their excellent work. Photography stylists Sondra Harrison Daniel, Charlisa Erwin Parker and Karen Smart Hall also deserve a special mention for the high quality of their collaboration with the photographers.

To the talented designers who helped create the following projects in this book, we extend a special word of thanks: The artwork for the Artwork Wall Hanging on page 30 was drawn by Katy Jones, the Anniversary Wall Hanging on page 31 was designed and crafted by Christina Tiano Myers and Cindy Tiano Jones and the projects for the Fireside Quilts section on pages 32-37 and the Friendship Gifts section on pages 38-41 were designed by Pat Sloan.